NEW GUINEA RESEARCH BULLETIN No. 52

CHIMBU FAMILY RELATIONSHIPS
IN PORT MORESBY

WHITEMAN

CHIMBU FAMILY RELATIONSHIPS
IN PORT MORESBY

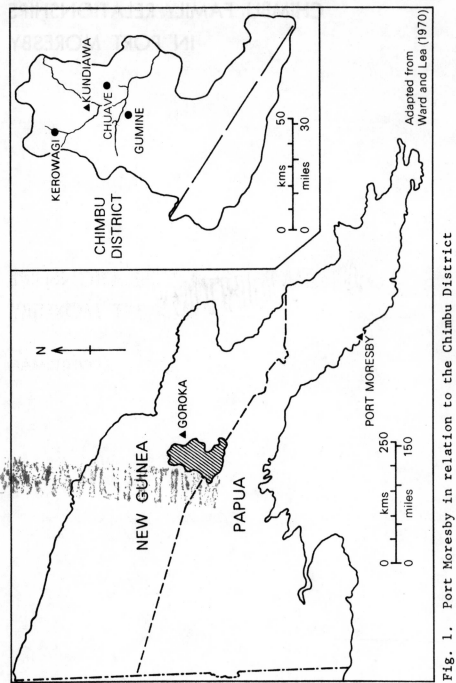

Fig. 1. Port Moresby in relation to the Chimbu District

New Guinea Research Bulletin no. 52

CHIMBU FAMILY RELATIONSHIPS IN PORT MORESBY

J. WHITEMAN

The New Guinea Research Unit
The Australian National University
Port Moresby and Canberra

Printed and manufactured in Australia by
The Australian National University

National Library of Australia
card no. and ISBN 0 85818 016 2

Library of Congress catalog
card no. 73-89536

Editor, New Guinea Research Bulletin
R. J. May

Manuscript editor
Susan Tarua

Contents

			Page
Preface			1
Chapter	1	Introduction	4
Chapter	2	The Chimbu: land and people	10
Chapter	3	Conjugal segregation and social networks of London and rural Chimbu families	39
Chapter	4	Social categories	43
Chapter	5	Social category I families	51
Chapter	6	Social category II families	76
Chapter	7	Social category III families	80
Chapter	8	Social networks of urban families	93
Chapter	9	Quantitative analysis of conjugal relationships - activities and behaviour	103
Chapter	10	Quantitative analysis of conjugal relationships - attitudes	117
Chapter	11	Summary and conclusions	135
Appendices		A Interview guide	147
		B Husband-wife division of labour	152
		C Case histories	154
Bibliography			172
Index			174
Tables			
4.1		Social category, secular education and income levels of twenty Chimbu families in Port Moresby	48
8.1		Formal relationships	97
8.2		Non-Chimbu relationships	100

		Page
9.1	Financial arrangements and mode of control	106
9.2	Domestic work	109
9.3	Abstinence from sexual intercourse	115
10.1	Attitudes relating to a good wife	118
10.2	Attitudes relating to a good husband	120
10.3	Attitudes to why people marry	122
10.4	Attitudes to husbands leaving wives in Chimbu during their long-term residence in Port Moresby	124
10.5	Attitudes to husbands sleeping in men's houses	126
10.6	Attitudes to polygyny	128
10.7	Attitudes to witchcraft	131
10.8	Attitudes to division of labour between husband and wife in Port Moresby	133

Figure

| 1 | Port Moresby in relation to the Chimbu District | Frontispiece |

Plates

1	A hamlet east of Chuave	12
2	A traditional woman's house	12
3	A woman placing hot stones in a mumu drum prior to cooking	19
4	This woman is using a traditional wooden digging-stick in her sweet potato garden	19
5	A girl emerging from confinement at the conclusion of her puberty ceremony	35
6	Houses in a shanty settlement	52
7	A low-covenant house	52
8	Card-playing is an important recreation in shanty settlements	54

		Page
9	Part of a compound household in a shanty settlement	56
10	Wives coming to Port Moresby find they must adapt to new forms of domestic life	56
11	Low-covenant houses in an army compound	77
12	High-covenant accommodation with all modern conveniences	82

Preface

In recent years there has been a great influx to Port Moresby
of people from other parts of Papua New Guinea, people who speak
a variety of languages, have different types of social organisation, and various amounts and kinds of contact with Western
society. The Chimbu, from the highlands of New Guinea, have
come in considerable numbers.

There are no records of when the first Chimbu came to live
in Port Moresby. They came as individuals rather than in groups,
each man finding his own way, by plane, to the city.[1] Until
1970 there were very few Chimbu women in Port Moresby, apart
from a small group of army wives, but since then the number of
both married and single women has increased greatly. However,
there are still many more Chimbu men than women in the city.

I had lived in the Chimbu in 1961-62 studying food habits,
and had observed family organisation and domestic life: the
separate men's houses and women's houses; the segregation of
and latent antagonism between the sexes; the children eating
and sleeping at one house one day and another the next; the
constant visiting of individuals and families; the enormous
food-exchanges involving a great expenditure of time and energy;
the day-to-day work of women in their gardens, looking after
pigs and cooking vegetables in stone ovens. It would be difficult to maintain such a way of life in the urban setting and I
was interested to see how Chimbu would adapt their family organisation and domestic life in Port Moresby.

There have been many family studies in Western, industrialised societies but few among tribal societies in urban areas.
I decided to base my research on a study that Bott (1971) made
in London, as her methods seemed suitable for use in Port
Moresby. Bott and a co-worker Robb carried out extensive
interviews with twenty London families and data were collected
about the organisation of family life, the husband-wife relation-

---

[1]Except for a few army recruits and labourers on rubber plantations about twenty-five miles away from the city. Some of
the latter have absconded to Port Moresby

1

ship and the relationships of these couples with others. From these data Bott (1971:60) developed the hypothesis that 'the degree of segregation in the role-relationship of husband and wife varies directly with the connectedness of the family's social network'. As with the London study, the present study of twenty Chimbu families is exploratory, with the aim of providing an insight into Chimbu family organisation and relationships in Port Moresby, as well as testing the applicability of Bott's concepts, methods and hypothesis to tribal societies in an urban environment. The research in Port Moresby was conducted in 1970-71.

Following an outline in Chapter 1 of the method of study, the material presented falls naturally into two parts. The first concerns traditional Chimbu marriage and domestic life, such as continues for the most part unchanged in the Chimbu today. This material, gathered by the participant-observation method in 1961-62, is presented in Chapter 2. It provides important background material for understanding and interpreting the second part, which describes urban Chimbu family relationships in Port Moresby. In Chapter 3 I discuss the differing characteristics of London and Chimbu families and their respective social networks. Chapter 4 explains my use of the term 'social category' as a means of classifying the families studied. Chapters 5, 6 and 7 describe the life-styles of families in the three different social categories. In Chapter 8 I summarise my findings about the social networks of the urban families. Chapter 9 attempts to quantify data collected about the activities and behaviour of husbands and wives. The problems of trying to quantify and tabulate these data are also discussed. In Chapter 10 I explore some of the attitudes of husbands and wives which are related to the degree of segregation in the husband-wife relationship. I present my conclusions about Chimbu conjugal relationships and social networks and the differences in these relationships between rural and urban families in Chapter 11.

Acknowledgments

This Bulletin is based on material presented in a thesis written in partial fulfilment of the requirements for a Master of Arts degree at the University of New South Wales in 1972. Much of the material was collected in association with my work in the Public Health Department of Papua New Guinea and I am indebted to the department for permission to publish it.

I am also indebted to Professor Congalton of the School of Sociology, University of New South Wales, for his valuable advice and suggestions during the writing of my thesis. The consequences of his assistance are reflected in the material in this Bulletin.

A very large debt is owed to those families who participated in the study, patiently replying to questions which often had no significance for them, and few of whom were in a position to understand the implications of my study. I hope that this work will in some small way contribute towards the understanding of the problems which Chimbu and other highlands families face when they migrate to cities such as Port Moresby.

Finally I would like to thank Susan Tarua for editing the material and assisting in the transformation of my thesis to its present form in this Bulletin.

Chapter 1

Introduction

Families in tribal societies

In tribal societies individuals live, work, marry and die
as members of a small group. For most men, particularly those
in patrilineal societies, this may be one continuing kin group
spanning their whole life; for women there may be two groups,
their natal kin group and the kin group of their husbands.
Within the group everyone knows one another and interacts in a
variety of roles. Each family may be cut off from social
relationships with people or groups outside of those kin
group(s) of which it, or one of its members, is a part. Bott
(1971:99) describes such families as being 'encapsulated'
within a kin group. By contrast, in Western, urban societies
many families have large, diffuse networks of social relationships involving many individuals and families from a wide geographic area each of whom interacts with the family of focus
in a limited number of roles. In such societies the family is
more highly 'individuated' than it is in tribal societies.[1]

In Papua New Guinea, as in many other developing countries,
tribal families are moving from a rural, traditional environment to an urban environment and individuals brought up in the
tribal environment are marrying and establishing families in
towns and cities. How does this affect the degree of individ-
uation of such families?

In most tribal societies there is a well-organised division
of labour between the sexes; within each sex-grouping individuals perform a variety of tasks. In Westernised, industrialised towns and cities the division of labour and specialisation

---

[1] 'Individuated' is used by Bott (1971:101) to describe the
degree to which 'the elementary family is separated off, differentiated out as a distinct and to some extent autonomous,
social group'.

of tasks and functions tend to be on an individual rather than
a purely sexual basis, and there is much greater specialisation
of economic roles. How does the tribal family in the urban
situation adapt to its new circumstances?

Port Moresby

Most indigenous people living in Port Moresby have a tribal
background. There were no towns or cities in Papua New Guinea
before Europeans arrived in the late nineteenth century; the
people lived instead in small villages or scattered hamlets or
homesteads. Sometimes they moved from site to site as old gardens were discarded and new ones made, or as a result of tribal
fighting.

In 1970 Port Moresby had a population of 56,206, of whom
42,616 were indigenous (Department of External Territories
1971:13). Initially most indigenous inhabitants were Papuans
but over the years more and more New Guineans have come across
the Owen Stanley Range to work in the city. Since 1966 the
number of highlanders, particularly Chimbu, has increased rapid-
ly. A few brought their families with them, but most were, and
still are, either single men or married men who have left their
wives and children in the highlands. Many of the latter have
lived without their families for over five years, a situation
which appears to cause them little concern.

Most Papua New Guineans in Port Moresby live in urbanised
ethnic villages (such as the Motu and Koitabu villages), in
shanty settlements made up of migrants, in houses or dormitories belonging to employers, or in low-cost rented houses.
A small number of more highly paid Papua New Guineans live in
intermediate and high-cost housing, their rent sometimes being
subsidised by their employer. Most army personnel live in individual low-cost homes within army compounds. My sample included families living in shanty settlements, in low-cost rented
houses, in low-cost houses belonging to employers, in army houses,
and in high-cost houses. These houses were in widely separated
parts of Port Moresby for it is a scattered city in relation to
its size, a factor which hinders social interaction between
people.

Selection of a tribal
group to study

For the purposes of a small-scale study of such a hetero-
genous population as exists in Port Moresby, it was thought
that a study of a single cultural group would control some of
the many variables which might otherwise mask trends or develop-
ments consequent on the urban situation. I selected the Chimbu

because I had spent time in their home area in 1961-62 and
because some of the contacts I made then were now living in
Port Moresby.

The Chimbu form one of the largest language groups in one
of the most densely populated parts of Papua New Guinea.
Migration to the urban areas will probably continue as a result of land shortages, tax payments, economic ambitions,
education, boredom with rural life, and fear of witchcraft.
As the number of Chimbu and other highlands groups in Port
Moresby and other urban areas in Papua New Guinea continues
to increase, so the need for studies of family organisation
and its adaptation to the urban environment increases. It is
hoped that this study has produced data of significance in the
understanding of some of the problems of tribal people, and of
Chimbu in particular, who come to live in the urban environment.

The sample

The sample of twenty Chimbu families was selected somewhat
arbitrarily, as was Bott's sample of twenty London families.
The aim was to include as many different types of family -
educated and non-educated, Lutheran, Catholic and pagan, shanty-
dwellers, low-cost-housing residents and high-covenant-housing
dwellers - as possible. The choice was limited because of the
small number of Chimbu families living in Port Moresby at the
time.

All the families studied, or the individuals which formed
them, had been geographically mobile. Most husbands had come
to Port Moresby first, followed by their wives and sometimes
children. Some had lived as a family in Chimbu before coming
to Port Moresby, others had lived elsewhere, while still others
had not been married until they, or their wives, came to the
city.

Traditional Chimbu life is egalitarian but in Port Moresby
different social strata are emerging. I viewed Chimbu society
in Port Moresby as being made up of three social categories.[1]
An attempt was made to find equal numbers of families for each
category but this proved to be impossible because there were
so few 'upper-class' (modern, sophisticated, Western-orientated -
none of these terms really seems appropriate) families, with
husbands who had received at least a few years of secondary
education and had skilled or professional employment. It was
almost as difficult to find families to put into an intermediary category, families in which the husband had semi-skilled

---

[1] See Chapter 4.

employment and had received a few years of primary schooling.[1]
The original criteria for classification of the families were
revised so that the categories finally used, and which I distinguish as I, II and III, are based on the family's style of
living rather than on the type of employment, income, or educational level of the husband.

In the final analysis the only real criterion, apart from
a willingness to assist me and the fact that the family was
living in Port Moresby, was that the husband and wife identified themselves with, or felt themselves to be, Chimbu. The
exception was a family where one partner was Chimbu and the
other came from a nearby highlands tribe.[2]

Method of selection

The selection of the sample spread out from two main contact points and one subsidiary one. The first source of contact was through two Gumine brothers living in Port Moresby
whom I had known when I was doing research near Gumine in
1961-62. They introduced me to a number of 'unsophisticated'
Chimbu families. The second main source of contact was a
young tertiary-educated Chimbu with whom I had kept in touch
since his student days. He introduced me to some of his
Chimbu friends and relatives, and to Chimbu families that he
had known when he was on the committee of the St Vincent de
Paul Society in Port Moresby. Most of the families contacted
by these two sources were either Roman Catholics or pagans
with Catholic leanings. In order to include some Lutheran
families in my sample - large numbers of Chimbu belong to the
Lutheran church and this mission's teachings relating to traditional customs differ somewhat from those of the Catholic
mission[3]- I was introduced by the mission to a Lutheran Chimbu.
Through him I was able to contact a number of Lutheran families.

---

[1] I could probably have found more army families that would
have fitted into the intermediary category, but in many respects family life in the army is not typical of the life of
people in the community at large, due to facilities supplied
and restrictions imposed upon soldiers and their families. I
therefore included only two army families in my sample.

[2] A Papuan husband who was included in the sample identified
himself as a Chimbu, and a number of Chimbu men stated that
they considered him to be one of them.

[3] See p.27.

The interview

Husbands and wives were sometimes interviewed together and sometimes separately. Sometimes they were alone, but more often other people were present. The interviews were unstructured but over a period of time all the points listed in the interview guide were covered for each couple.[1]

My explanations of the study, as well as the wording of the questions, varied from family to family due to the varied backgrounds of the people involved. Bott and Robb were concerned with keeping their interviews as uniform as possible (Bott 1971:17-24). I did not consider this to be so important and would describe my interviews as having taken place for the most part within the social context of the families concerned.

Interviews were conducted in either English or Pidgin,[2] and were tape-recorded. Initially I tried working with an interpreter but sometimes the interviews were not relaxed due to the Chimbu's suspicion of strangers from other parts of Chimbu, or because of the difficulty of some people speaking a different dialect to that of the interpreter. I found it more satisfactory to work without an interpreter.

My relationship with the families, some of whom I had known for years, was one of informal friendliness, particularly with the wives. Some of the husbands spent very little time in their homes, so I did not have an opportunity to get to know them well.

There were no set schedules for the interviews, and no set number of interviews to be given. I stopped interviewing but continued to make casual visits when I had all the basic information I wanted, or thought that I would be able to get, from interviews on those aspects of life covered by the interview guide. There was some overlapping of questions in the different sections, this being useful in checking the consistency of the replies.

Interview guide

The information collected was classified under the following headings:

---

[1] See Appendix A.

[2] Only one person could speak neither of these languages, although many New Guinean women are hesitant to speak in Pidgin in the presence of men.

Topic I: Port Moresby residence
Topic II: Marital and family status
Topic III: Husband's activities and attitudes
Topic IV: Wife's activities and attitudes
Topic V: Social relationships

Except for social relationships, each topic was divided
into two sections, A and B. Part A was for recording replies
to questions about what people said that they did or thought,
and part B was where comments about people's attitudes on
certain matters relating to the topics were listed, if I felt
that I had adequate information to do so. I attempted to distinguish between attitudes that were expressed and those that
were my interpretations, and also to distinguish between
attitudes and behaviour.

The analysis

The information collected from the families was analysed in
terms of segregation/jointness[1] in the husband-wife relationship and in terms of the density and composition of the family's
social networks. An attempt was made to do this both quali-
tatively and quantitatively, but the information on social networks was not sufficiently detailed for quantitative analysis.
I obtained sufficient data to make a general description of
each couple's social network, of whom the couple visited and
who visited them, and of their contacts with people in the
Chimbu, but I did not investigate in detail the content and
frequency of these relationships. I could therefore make only
a qualitative analysis of each family's social network.

---

[1] See pp. 39-40.

Chapter 2

The Chimbu: land and people

Definition

The name 'Chimbu' is sometimes used inaccurately to describe anyone who comes from the eastern half of the New Guinea
highlands; it should be applied only to those people who speak
the Kuman language, or a dialect of this language, and who come
from the area which now forms the major part of the Chimbu
District (see Fig. 1). Only since Europeans came to the area
in the 1930s have these people used the term 'Chimbu' to describe themselves. I use the term to include all those people
who now call themselves Chimbu, and who feel that they have
something in common with other people who call themselves
Chimbu which they do not have with people who do not consider
themselves Chimbu. For some people who speak Kuman dialects
their use of the term 'Chimbu' depends upon to whom they are
talking: when talking to people from outside the highlands
they call themselves Chimbu; when talking to people from other
parts of the Chimbu they may call themselves Elimbaris, Chuaves
or Sinasinas. People from the area referred to as Chimbu by
Brookfield and Brown,[1] which I refer to as the 'Chimbu proper',
have only one name for themselves, 'Chimbu'.

My sample includes families from near Chuave, from Sinasina
and from Gumine, as well as from 'Chimbu proper'. The Sinasina people live to the southeast of Kundiawa, the District
headquarters. Prior to the 1930s there was no Sinasina place
or people. It is a term which early Administration officers
used for convenience when referring to the people in this
particular area.[2] The Gumine people, south of the Waghi River,

---

[1] By the Chimbu we mean about 55,000 people who speak the main
Chimbu language, live north of the Waghi River, and occupy
the northern half of the Chimbu Subdistrict and some adjacent
areas of the Minj Subdistrict of the Western Highlands District. (Brookfield and Brown 1963:3).

[2] Personal communication: R. Hide, 1971.

10

consider themselves to be 'second-class' Chimbu, and they are looked down upon by the Chimbu to the north. But they do consider themselves to be Chimbu, and they are considered to be Chimbu by the people in 'Chimbu proper'.

Customs and character

As far as is known, there has never been a single, large-scale political unit of Chimbu. The people form a loosely knit collection of social groups who speak the same language and practise some customs which they feel differentiate them from their neighbours. There are dialect differences in various parts of the Kuman-speaking area and variations in customs and beliefs both within and between dialect groups. These differences, which are readily perceived by anthropologists working in the area, may be unnoticed or unimportant to the Chimbu themselves. This may be in part because until recently there was little contact between the people of different parts of Chimbu, and also because these differences seem minor compared with the differences between Chimbu and Papuan or European customs and beliefs.

East of the Chimbu River highlanders live in villages or hamlets; to the west they live in scattered homesteads, a change which appears to be associated not with differences in dialect but with differences in behavioural norms.[1] I was last in Chimbu in 1967. At that time, driving along the twisting, bumping Highlands Highway between Chuave and Kerowagi, usually in a Landrover, crossing ravines on rough wooden bridges, plunging into sudden, thick banks of mist, or skirting a landslide only inches from a precipice on one side, the observer could note, a few miles east of Kundiawa, the sudden absence of hamlets of round, low-roofed, thatched houses strung out along narrow ridges of high land, and see instead only single houses, scattered alongside a sweet potato garden or in a patch of kunai grass. In recent years some missions and local government councils have encouraged people in the western part of the Chimbu (and possibly in parts of the Western Highlands) to build their houses in villages instead of in individual gardens. I do not know how successful this has been but in 1967 I did see one new village near Gumine.

---

[1] Hatanaka (1972:8) states that after 1940 the Lutheran mission in the Sinasina area established villages comprised of strings of hamlets. This is not completely in accordance with information given to me by Chimbu people from the western part of the Chimbu who suggested that traditionally, in the eastern part of Chimbu, a group of women's houses were built around a central men's house, situated on a ridge of high land.

12

Plate 1. A hamlet east of Chuave. The building in the foreground is not in traditional style.

Plate 2. A traditional woman's house.

The Chimbu are often described as being aggressive, quarrel-some people, but hard workers.[1] They are also sometimes called the 'Scotsmen of the Territory', no doubt because of their strong economic motivation and their tendency to accumulate rather than spend wealth (in fact, it is long-term, small saving interspersed with sudden, large-scale, lavish spending). Oram (1968:269) says of the Hula that there is an economic element in every social relationship, and this is also true of the Chimbu. In fact, it may be more pronounced among the Chimbu because of their great drive and initiative, and their strong desire to work for economic gain. One of my Chimbu informants in Port Moresby said, 'The Chimbu never give anything for nothing, not even food'. This is no doubt true, but the Chimbu remembers what he owes as well as what he is owed, and in contrast to his apparent avarice he is also proud to be generous and to be able to make large presentations. I found the Chimbu individualistic and pragmatic, but also very kind and emotional, with a keen sense of justice, a justice related to his own social mores.

Leadership among the Chimbu is achieved not ascribed; individuals or groups can readily break off their allegiance to one group or leader and align with another if they feel that it is in their interest to do so. Blood and birth by no means fix forever a man's place and status in society and although blood ties are important, people can readily be adopted into a group with which they have no known blood ties. Such people are treated in the same way as blood members of the group. This system is probably a consequence of continual fighting in the past between clans and even clan sections, and the need to maintain a group's manpower so that it could defend its rights against others. By 1961 fighting on a large or continuous scale, usually over land or pigs or women, had ceased.

Decisions among men are made through consensus after discussion; women have no direct say in community, group or family affairs except in those matters considered to be in their special sphere of interest (e.g., the cultivation of sweet potatoes, some types of magic, antenatal care). In these

---

[1] Possibly this aggressiveness is related to the Chimbu system of sexual relationships (see pp. 29-33). Fighting, quarrelling, the excited speeches made at food-exchanges, may all be socialised means of sublimating the sexual drive, particularly among men. Economic avarice, in the modern or traditional context, may also be an aspect of this phenomenon.

spheres they make their own decisions; joint decisions with men, or consultation with men other than on an individual basis, are unusual.

When I arrived at Wandi, four miles west of Kundiawa, in 1961 coffee had been introduced but was only just coming into production. It had not yet been introduced at Gumine when I went to live there some months later. Wandi people earned a little money selling sweet potatoes and other vegetables at Kundiawa. Husbands kept the money they earned from selling their crops (bananas and sugar cane) and women kept their earnings from the sale of sweet potatoes, green leaves and other root crops they had planted, tended and harvested.

Most people at that time owned a bush knife, a kitchen knife, a spoon and fork, a pair of shorts or a loose blouse, and a strip of cotton material worn as a laplap. In spite of these innovations, life was basically the traditional stone-age one. Gardening and cooking techniques had changed but little. Gift-exchanges, reciprocal obligations and the search for prestige were the main foci of life. The production and exchange of pigs and pig meat were of prime importance to all social groupings. Records of debts and obligations were maintained with small pieces of wood; the jaws of pigs received were kept and strung up between trees; knots were made in lengths of rope, and sooner or later every gift was reciprocated.

'Chimbuland'

The Chimbu country is mountainous, with steep, deep valleys containing fast-flowing rivers that are often difficult to cross. In the far west is the beginning of the great, wide grassland valley of the Waghi River.

Sweet potatoes are the staple food and grow on even the steepest mountain slopes. Bananas, taro, various green leaf vegetables, pumpkins and beans are other important food crops. After being cultivated for approximately two years, land is left fallow for about seven years, varying according to the particular area and population density.[1] There is no real forest land, the only large trees being at sacred places, such as the areas used for holding pig festivals. These plots of land are never cultivated.

---

[1] The large-scale cultivation of coffee during the 1960s may have changed the cycle of land usage.

Transportation in Chimbu is difficult. The Highlands Highway, unsealed, twisting and narrow, is often blocked or swept
away by landslides after torrential rain. The side-roads are
even more tortuous and unreliable. For the Chimbu, walking is
still the usual way to get from one place to another.

There are about twenty airstrips in Chimbu, some owned by
missions and some by the government. There is no road link
between Chimbu and Port Moresby and people have to fly back
and forth. Some Chimbu have flown to Port Moresby or Kundiawa
but have never travelled in a car.

Domestic life

Chimbu domestic life is pervaded by the dichotomy, even
antagonism, between the sexes that is characteristic of highlands societies (Meggitt 1964). This antagonism seems to be
more marked among the western tribes than the eastern, the
Chimbu being in the centre geographically.

There have been considerable changes in Chimbu domestic
life in recent years. The following describes the basic pattern of most people in 1961 and 1962. Some changes had already
begun at that time, particularly in Wandi, but many others have
developed since as a result of education and increasing adaptation to a cash economy.

Traditionally, Chimbu wives live in houses near their
gardens,[1] with their daughters and young sons. In the men's
houses there live from five to fifteen men of the subclan section, plus any who have been adopted into it. A group of men's
houses is associated with a subclan, within which many joint
activities are carried out, such as marriage payments, gardening, or building a house on the ceremonial ground for use at a
pig festival. Members of the subclan help a man to build
houses for his wife or wives, and support him in disputes with
outsiders; they try to settle peacefully any disputes between
members of the subclan.

The men explain that they live in separate houses from
their wives because of their traditional preoccupation with
tribal fighting. Fighting was not the concern of the women,
who were required to do their gardening and other duties. It
seems that women were not often deliberately killed in these
fights, even though they lived unprotected; they might, how-

---

[1] East of the Chimbu River women's houses are built around
the men's houses, forming small hamlets of members of one subclan (see p.11, fn.1).

ever, be captured and taken as wives. Men, I was told, have
many things to discuss among themselves that are not the concern of women, including pig festivals, ceremonial food-
exchanges and marriage payments, and they do not wish to live
in close association with women.

The domestic life of the husband is centred around the
men's house, while that of the wife is centred round her own
individual house. East of the Chimbu River these two houses
are situated close together but in other areas the husband
might live half-an-hour's walk away from his wife's house.
There is less domestic segregation between husband and wife
in the east than in the west. This accords with the increasing dichotomy between highlands men and women and the aggress-
ion and fear that men further west express towards women
(Meggitt 1964:221), although there are exceptions to this
trend.[1]

Men's houses and women's houses are built of the same
materials but are of different design. Both have wooden poles
for the frame, a double row of wooden boards with dry kunai
grass stuffed between them for walls, and a thatched roof of
kunai grass. Men's houses are built on a high piece of land
for strategic purposes. Inside is a single dormitory-like
room with sloping beds parallel to each long side and a central passageway between doorways at each end. There are no
windows, the only light coming in from the two doorways.
There are no chimneys: smoke from a number of open wood fires
in the central passageway simply seeps through the roof.

Women's houses have three 'rooms' inside. There is only
one door to the house, leading into a sitting area which is
also used for cooking when it rains. In the 'Chimbu proper'
this room is in the centre of the house, with the cubicles
where pigs sleep on one side of it, and the sleeping area for
women and children on the other side.[2] In Gumine the sitting
area is at one end of the house, and a passage from it leads
past the pigs' cubicles on either side to the sleeping area
at the far end. There are no windows and these houses are

---

[1] Strathern (1972:295-314), in discussing the relationship
between husband and wife in the Melpa-speaking tribes near
Mt Hagen, indicates that there may be a closer relationship
between the sexes there than among the Kuma to the east.

[2] Pigs are naturally house-trained from an early age and do
not foul the house. They may, however, harbour lice.

built low on the ground for warmth.[1] The floor is covered
with dead leaves and dry grass, which is added to from time
to time but seldom, if ever, replaced.

Women, daughters and young sons sleep on kunai grass strewn
on the floor, on a pandanus mat on the grass or sometimes on
a grey woollen blanket bought at the tradestore. Men sleep
on the bare boards of their beds or cover them with a pandanus
mat or grey blanket. People sit cross-legged on the beds or
on the kunai grass on the floor of the house.

Each morning at dawn the wife or an elder daughter gets up
and puts some sweet potatoes into the ashes of the fire,
which has been burning slowly all night. Then she takes the
pigs to an old garden to forage in all day, gets her string
basket ready to take to the garden, or sits and breastfeeds
a young child.

It is usually cool, and the women and children sit around
the fire waiting for the potatoes to cook. Some women wear a
loose cotton blouse, faded and mud-stained, but most wear only
a small pubic apron in front and some strips of bark cloth or
black cotton material tucked over the 'g'-string at the back.
Little girls from about the age of one year wear the same type
of apron, and boys from about two years wear a 'g'-string with
a small pubic scarf tucked in the front of it. Traditionally
these scarves, which the men wore too, were crocheted by the
women from home-made string and possum fur. A few springs of
leaves were tucked in the 'g'-string at the back. Today, for
everyday use, cheap cotton material bought at the tradestore
is often worn in place of the crocheted scarf and shorts are
becoming popular with younger men.

The husband either cooks his own 'breakfast' from sweet
potatoes his wife left at the men's house the evening before,
or one of his children brings him (and any of his sons who
slept in the men's house that night) some cooked ones from
his wife's house. Until about 9 o'clock he and the other men
usually discuss their day's activities, after which they
either go off together or he may join his wife at her house
or in the garden. He might go to a new garden he is preparing or walk down to the nearest mission or government station
to look for a little excitement.

-----

[1] At Wandi in 1961 a few people built coastal-type houses on
stilts, about a foot off the ground, with plaited reed floors
and walls and a fire area covered with mud or a piece of metal
sheeting. The Chimbu found these houses cold, and they
caught fire easily.

The wife meantime shuts up her house (in earlier days she might have put a spell on the door to frighten people from entering while she is away) and goes off to the garden with her daughters and small sons. Sometimes she goes with a neighbour who will, through marriage or blood, be related to her; sometimes her husband goes with her and the children, or he meets them in the garden; sometimes she goes alone with the children. She may take one or more small pigs with her, and perhaps a dog.

The garden may be close to the house, or a mile or so away up steep hills and across ravines, each woman usually having more than one garden plot. As the day goes on the sun becomes hot, and Chimbu say that they do not wash often or go without pig's grease on their skins because this protects them from being burnt by the sun.[1] They plant, weed and harvest in the same way that their ancestors did, although magic growth-promoting spells and spells to prevent people stealing crops, may be omitted. A bush-knife is used to weed instead of the wooden stick of the past, but the women still do much of the work with their bare hands.

In the early afternoon the women gather food for the evening meal: sweet potatoes, green leaves, and possibly some beans, taro, tapioca or other vegetables, all of which they wash in a stream on the way home. They collect firewood and carry it in another string bag slung across their head, or they may make a special trip for it later, when they fetch the pigs.

Once home, the wife begins to cook the evening meal. Usually she chops her own firewood, but if her husband has brought back a heavy log he may chop it up for her. Most families have a steel-headed axe these days.

Food is cooked in an earth oven or hollowed-out wooden drum, or is boiled.[2] For cooking in an earth oven (mumu) special heat-retaining stones are heated by burning over an open fire. The green leaves are wrapped in banana leaves for cooking, and root vegetables are usually peeled. The hot stones are picked up carefully with bamboo tongs, placed in the wooden drum or in a depression in the ground, and covered with banana leaves. Food is arranged on these leaves according

---

[1] At these high altitudes only 4° from the equator, the skin is very quickly burnt.

[2] The saucepan is a recently introduced domestic item, but leaves were, and still are, sometimes boiled in a bamboo segment.

Plate 3. A woman placing hot stones in a mumu
drum prior to cooking.

Plate 4. This woman is using a traditional wooden
digging-stick in her sweet potato garden. The fence
would have been constructed by her husband's clansmen.

to the amount of time required for cooking and then covered with more leaves, stones and leaves. Sometimes all this is covered with an old sack or damp soil.

Small, inferior sweet potatoes for the pigs are cooked in the same manner, either in the same mumu as the family's food or in a separate one if there are many pigs to feed. Looking after pigs is a very important part of a wife's responsibilities. Most women have two or three pigs of their own, as well as some of their husbands' to look after. They are regarded as pets, and a family does not eat its own pigs; they are eventually given away to others, sometimes with genuine grief, at a food-exchange gathering.

Any children or visitors present when the food is being served sit on logs or banana leaves and eat the solid pieces of root vegetables or bundles of leaves with their fingers. If the husband is in the men's house some food will be sent to him wrapped in leaves; he will share it with his children and some of the other men. A good wife provides food for her husband's relatives in addition to her immediate family. A mother does not worry if her children are not with her or her husband at mealtimes: she knows that they will be eating with a kinswoman nearby.

Married men spend some time working in the garden or making houses for their wives or their own men's house. They are more active than single men in the lengthy discussions about gift-exchanges, land problems and ceremonial activities, but many of these discussions now have less significance than they did in the past. With the cessation of tribal warfare life has become rather dull for the average Chimbu man. This may in part account for the great popularity of gambling, and for the ever-increasing number of men leaving to work on plantations or in the towns.

Marriage

In 1961-62 polygyny was not as widely practised as it used to be, probably as a result of strong mission opposition (Brown 1969:92). Although in the past it was the ideal state of marriage, only a few older men of status, usually fight leaders, were able to achieve it. Today, economic assets are important in enabling a man to have more than one wife, and sometimes masculine charm is also a factor.[1]

---

[1] In 1972 Chimbu in Port Moresby said that many young girls were marrying old but wealthy men, i.e., ones with trucks and businesses, regardless of whether they had other wives. They

To be a polygynist, a man must be a hard worker as he will
have to prepare land for his wives' gardens, or have something
to give to kinsmen who help him in the garden or in building
his wives' houses. Each wife lives in her own house with her
children and pigs. She expects to be able to live the same
life as if she is the only wife. If it is to be a peaceful
arrangement any additional wives must be acceptable to the
first wife. Sometimes a wife wants her husband to have more
wives (Barnett 1970: appendix 3D), sometimes she does not.
Sometimes she does not like a particular woman that her husband wishes to marry. However, if after several years of
marriage a wife has not had any children, she is in a very
weak position to reject her husband's proposed addition.
Should she refuse, her husband would probably divorce her and
demand the return of his brideprice because it was believed
that the woman was at fault if there were no children.

All Christian missions working in the Chimbu condemn polygyny, and as polygynists cannot become church members[1] a number
of leading men have been denied membership. For the Chimbu
one of the most significant aspects of Christian teaching is
the rule: one man, one wife.

The only men who do not marry are maimed or mentally defec-
tive. Socially a man is not an adult until he is married,
and if he is unmarried in middle age he would be an object of
jest. Spinsters are unknown (Brown 1969:92). Widows and
divorcees are encouraged to marry again, and indeed, according to one of my interpreters (a Chimbu woman who had divorced
her non-Chimbu husband), a woman has to be married because she
needs a husband to build her a house and prepare the ground
for her gardens.[2]

---

1 (cont'd)
did not mention the fact that with an increasing number of
young men working and living outside the Chimbu, young marriage partners for girls in the Chimbu might be limited. A
number of young men in Port Moresby have been married in
absentia to girls in the Chimbu.

[1] In some missions (none of these were in Chimbu in 1962)
husbands may retain the wives they already have before applying for church membership, but may not take any additional
wives.

[2] In the case of dire necessity, a brother would probably help
his sister, but the brother's wife might not be very happy
about the situation.

Marriage in the Chimbu is basically a group-instigated, group-performed and group-maintained relationship, although there are many exceptions to the group-instigated aspect. Even in 1961 it was hard to assess what influence missions had on these exceptions. Many missionaries are strongly opposed to arranged marriages, but often marriages are only 'arranged' after the couple, the girl in particular, have indicated that they are interested in marrying each other.

Mate-selection and marriage

The following is an outline of the ideal traditional Chimbu marriage rather than an actual marriage.

The kinsmen of a young man of about twenty-four years of age decide that it is time he married. They begin to collect feathers, shells, stone-axes or money, pieces of opossum fur and other valuables for 'paying for a wife' for him. This 'payment', brideprice, or bridewealth as it is sometimes called, serves a number of purposes,[1] probably the most important of which, for the Chimbu, is to establish friendship and initiate exchange relationships, which are positive evidences of friendship, between the subclan sections of the woman and the man. Sometimes a man's kinsmen have a particular women in mind when they start collecting valuables, but sometimes they take the brideprice around, or let it be known in the men's houses what valuables they have, until they find a group which has a suitable woman and is willing to accept their brideprice. The choice of who shall marry who lies with the women's agnatic kin group rather than the man's group because it is the former who decides whether to accept the offer made by the man's group. According to Brown (1964: 339), either the man or the woman on behalf of whom the marriage transactions are being made can refuse to marry or stop the marriage proceeding, but in practice most accede to the wishes of their kin. Barnett (1970:appendix 3D) cites a case of a woman who ran away in the middle of the main marriage ceremony.

The rules of exogamy for the Chimbu are, like many of their rules of behaviour, open to manipulation according to circum-

---

[1] A leading Gumine man, on learning that in European custom men do not, at least directly, pay for their brides, commented, 'Europeans cannot think much of their wives if they do not pay for them!' Chimbu value their wives in terms of their economic and procreative contributions to their lineage group.

stance. Men are forbidden to marry into their mother's subclan group, although this is not a formally constituted group;
however, they do sometimes marry women in this group (Brown
1969:82). They may not marry women in their own clan as they
are regarded as sisters. After a woman marries, her natal
group expects to receive a bride in return sometime in the
future, but this is never a direct exchange.

Once the two groups of kinsmen agree, the woman may stay
with the man's mother for a few weeks. There she is closely
scrutinised by her prospective mother-in-law, who will decide
whether she will make a suitable wife for her son: whether
she works hard and is respectful to her prospective affines,
or whether she is lazy and insolent. After marriage the
young wife will be living among her husband's kinsmen, so it
is important that they should approve of her, and in particular that she is approved of by the mother-in-law, on whom she
will have to depend for so many things in the early months
of her married life. If the prospective mother-in-law does
not think that the woman is suitable as a wife, she will be
decorated with paint and feathers and sent back home. The
man's agnates will then have to look for another bride.

Brown (1964:334 and 1969:83, and Barnett (1970:87) probably following Brown) does not consider a woman living with the
man's mother to be married at this stage, although Brown says
that the men themselves talk as if they are. (I am not clear
whether she means they talk this way when the woman is staying with the man's mother, or whether she means that in
retrospect they talk this way.) When talking about their
own marriage histories, some of my Port Moresby informants
referred to their marriages to women who were later decorated
with feathers and sent back home. In most cases these
'marriages' had not been consummated, but consummation does
not seem to be a criterion of marriage in Chimbu society.
In fact, both before and for some weeks after 'marriage' the
man and woman often avoid each other.[1] Barnett (1970:91)
suggests that this is so that the young man shall not be
judged to be overly anxious for a close relationship with a
woman. He suggests that it is the ceremonial eating of pork
by the man and woman at the payment ceremony that indicates
a marriage has taken place. However, when a woman has been
married before, this part of the marriage ceremony is omitted
from succeeding marriages, a fact which tends to contradict
Barnett's suggestion.

---

[1] For a discussion of the significance of sexual intercourse
in Chimbu society, see pp.30-2, 37, and 114-6.

Once a woman has been accepted by her future affines, marriage preparations begin in earnest by both the bride's and the groom's natal groups, and these activities are now extended beyond their immediate subclan sections. Pigs are killed and cooked, and pork exchanged. The night before the wedding exchange the woman will return home if she is still living with the man's people, and the groom's subclansmen and other relatives, with their wives and children, will go and listen to the bride's subclan telling her about her marital responsibilities, emphasising the importance of working hard and providing food for her husband's kinsmen. She is told not to visit her natal group too often or for too long (although it is expected that she will visit her family sometimes) and not to hang about the government station (Brown 1969:85).

The following day the brideprice is brought on a special display board to the bride's home, and public speeches are delivered about the friendly relationship which now exists between the two kin groups. In the exchanges that follow, almost as much is given to the man's group by the woman's group as vice versa. This exchange is followed by the eating of pork livers by the bride and groom if the bride has not been married before.

At the marriage ceremonies I witnessed near Gumine three aspects in particular impressed me. One was the care with which the bride's relatives examined the brideprice, even measuring the large shells against lengths of twine. This was followed by speeches from the bride's kinsmen who routinely, I was told, complain that there are not enough valuables, this in turn being followed by a mock quarrel between the two parties. This would seem to be an institutionalised, overt expression of the importance of economic gain, or economic parity - I find it impossible to judge which is the more correct description - for the Chimbu. There is no shame, no hyprocrisy, about being interested in material or ceremonial wealth or reciprocity.

Another impression was that of the sadness exhibited by the bride's parents and other relatives. At one ceremony the father slashed his ear lobes with a razor as a sign of his great grief at losing his daughter. Mothers sat quietly weeping, their faces and bodies covered in mud similar to that used for mourning. Female relatives threw themselves on the ground, sobbing loudly. Whether or not this was convention or genuine grief[1] is not important sociologically; its

---

[1] Fathers have such little contact with their daughters, particularly after they have reached puberty, that it is difficult to believe their emotional attachment to them can compare with that of their wives.

sociological significance lies in the fact that here was an expressed sense of sorrow at the loss of a daughter, a relative,
a member of the social group, rather than an expression of joy
for the individual woman's happiness in her new life.[1]

The third aspect of Chimbu weddings that impressed me was
the lack of focus on the two individuals being married. Most
of the time they were in the background, indiscernible from
the crowd, and never together. As mentioned, for the Chimbu,
marriage, that is the formalities associated with it, is a
group-instigated and group-performed activity, although this
does not preclude the individuals directly concerned from
taking an active part in the informal aspects.

On the day after the 'wedding' the groom's subclan cooks
food for the bride's kinsmen, and in ceremonies in the Gumine
area (which may be different in some respects to other parts
of the Chimbu) the bride formally opens a mumu and takes out
some of the cooked food. This indicates to everyone present
that she is now a working member of her husband's social
group, cooking and distributing food as a member of his group
and not of her own natal group. From now on the bride must
work hard, helping her mother-in-law and her husband's kinswomen. In due course she is given her own plot of land to
plant, and her husband will build a house for her. In the
meantime she lives with her husband's mother. Her days of
wandering about with female companions,[2] simply enjoying life
and taking part in courting parties and singing evenings, are
now over. She is a married woman. However, a married woman
is frequently married several times before she finally settles
down, which often is not until she has had a child.

A successful marriage is followed by exchanges, visits and
gifts between the agnates of the bride and groom. After each
birth a formal gift is made to the bride's natal group, and
her children often stay with their matrilateral kin. Her
parents or siblings may stay with her for months, or a young
girl of the bride's natal group come to keep her company, for

---

[1] Brown (1969:90) points out the difficult period of adjust-
ment that a young Chimbu wife has during the first months of
married life: the sadness of leaving her natal kin group and
adjusting to a new group of people, her husband's kin, with
whom, in many instances, she has had little or no previous
contact.

[2] See p.34.

they think that she might be lonely without any of her kin.[1]
In the Chimbu a married woman has economic, political and
legal ties with her husband's kin group, but her emotional
ties are with her natal group and with her own children, who
form part of her husband's patrilineage.

The type of marriage here described is a model only, and
there are many variations both between the different areas
of Chimbu, and between different couples.[2] Brown (1964:339)
suggests that only rarely do young people choose their own
marriage partner,[3] but it is difficult to obtain statistics
on this and there is sometimes only a very fine distinction
between persuasion and suggestion, or between a suggestion
that is willingly accepted and one that is grudgingly acceded
to. The distinction between an arranged marriage and a free-
choice marriage is not always clear cut.

There are many institutionalised activities where young
Chimbu people of both sexes can meet and become attracted to
one another. For this reason it is difficult to believe that
marriages initiated by the partners themselves, or by one of
the partners, are not as much a norm as is the system described above.

Reay (1959:176-7) reports similar social activities involving single girls and boys and men among the Kuma, to the west
of Chimbu. According to Reay (1959:178), the friendships
formed during these activities are not intended to lead to
marriage, for a young girl must marry the man her kin have
selected. Frequently the girls protest very vigorously, but
it seems, to no avail. I have not heard about or witnessed
such protesting in the Chimbu, probably because girls can
stop the wedding at any time by walking out (Brown 1964:339).[4]

I suggest that among the Chimbu, provided socially recognised rules of exogamy are not violated, free choice of marriage partner is available traditionally and occurs frequently today. The various occasions where single girls and boys

---

[1] This seems to indicate that at least in the early stages,
marriage is not expected to provide adequate companionship
and emotional satisfaction for the wife.

[2] See Appendix C for examples.

[3] In a later paper Brown (1969:95) indicates that free choice
of marriage partner is accepted practice among Chimbu.

[4] Strathern (1972:88) reports that a Melpa woman can refuse
to marry a man if she wishes.

and men meet together can be regarded as courting or precourt-
ing activities. Married women do not take part in them, and
the fact that married men do, does not in a polygynous society
mean that some of the friendships generated on these occasions
are not expected to lead to marriage. However, if the man's
mother or an existing wife objects to the woman chosen it
might be difficult for the man to persuade his agnates to pay
brideprice.

The Catholic mission in Chimbu condemns arranged marriages
and tells its members that young people should be allowed to
choose their own partners. Most missions are also against
many of the traditional occasions where young people meet and
become attracted to one another. Indeed, Chimbu Lutherans
told me that they were not allowed to participate in such
activities, but not all young people accepted this ruling.[1]

Young people from different places can meet together and
form attachments on a number of important occasions. The
large pig festivals held every five to seven years provide an
opportunity for men and single girls from friendly clans to
meet. Married women do not attend these festivals. Elope-
ments are expected at each festival, but before one can be
considered as a marriage the couple will have to consult
their respective kinsmen, who, if they agree to the marriage
will prepare for pig and food-exchanges. This may take some
time if the boy's clan was host at the festival as its stock
of pigs will have been depleted and supplies of vegetables
may also be short.

The small, informal 'turning head' parties, and the larger
singing and caressing parties, are attended by single girls
and married or single men.[2] At the 'turning head' parties,
the men sit in two rows, back to back, in the centre of the
sitting area in a woman's house. The girls sit opposite them,
along the walls. The room is crowded and hot. The only
light comes from the flickering flames of an open fire. The
men and girls croon continuously, rolling their heads from
side to side. Sometimes they lean forward and press their
forehead against that of the person opposite, continuing to

---

[1] Some villages or clan-groupings that were originally Lutheran transferred their allegiance to the Catholic mission
because they did not want to give up traditional activities
banned by the Lutherans.

[2] As far as I know, none has ever taken place in Port Moresby.
Some young men tried to organise one in 1973 but only three
girls arrived to take part in it.

move their heads from side to side. Every now and again the
men move along one place so that they sit opposite another
girl. This activity is said to be sexually satisfying.

When I was living in Wandi a party of young men hired a
truck to go to a large singing and caressing party that they
had been invited to by the girls of a clan some miles away.
These, like the 'turning head' parties, go on for most of the
night. When the singing stops, the girls and men sleep together in the house, but sexual intercourse should not take
place. Chaperones may be present as a precaution.[1]

Divorce

If a couple are divorced, the children remain with the
father unless it is socially recognised that the husband is
to blame for the breakdown of the marriage, by openly neglect-
ing his duties as a husband for some time. Brideprice would
probably not be returned to him, although this would depend
to some extent on circumstances.

In Sinasina ownership of children is more equally balanced
between husband and wife than it is in other parts of the
Chimbu. Divorced women are more likely to be allowed to keep
at least one of their children. However, public opinion as
to blame still influences who receives custody of the children.
For many Gumine men talking in abstract terms, it was incon-
ceivable that a husband could be blamed for a marriage breakdown: it was always the woman's fault, and as they would not
want children to be brought up by an irresponsible woman, the
children should stay with their father! However, by 1967
some women were realising that in their disputes with their
husbands they would gain a more sympathetic hearing at the
sub-district office than at the traditional Chimbu courts comprised of married men. Consequently women began to take
serious marital disputes to the Administration for settlement.[2]

Brideprice and children are stabilising factors in marriage.
A mother is loath to leave her husband as she will probably

---

[1] A similar situation occurred in a number of other Papua New
Guinea societies; in northern Europe and the northeastern
United States the practice of 'bundling' was common until the
eighteenth century (Fielding 1942: chapter 4).

[2] At least one Administration officer blamed marital disputes
on the custom of separate houses for husbands and wives. He
told people in his court hearings that a husband and wife
should live together in the same house.

lose her children (or at least some of them). Her kinsmen will be unhappy because unless her husband is recognised as the guilty party, which rarely occurs, they will have to re-pay the brideprice they received for her. However, the re-payment will be reduced if she is leaving children with the husband. If the woman goes directly to another husband, he will have to compensate the previous husband rather than her kinsmen.

Sexual practices and attitudes

The antagonism between men and women in the highlands is expressed in different ways in different tribes, but always there is some institutionalised method of overcoming the con-flict which results from the man's fear of a woman, or rather his fear of her sexuality, and his need for a woman to satis-fy his sexual desires, to provide him with children, and to perform certain tasks for him. He believes that too much con-tact with women will weaken a man and spoil his skin, as well as spread diseases. Menstrual blood might harm him or his crops. Given the opportunity, women might usurp the power of men in society. Women are more likely to have supernatural powers (that is, be witches), and make trouble for men, than are men.

Women need men to give them children, to provide them with houses, to break in the ground for new gardens, and to make fences around the gardens. I never heard women talk dispar-agingly of men, but on many occasions men indicated that they had little respect for women in general, saying 'Women are nothing. They only make string bags and look after children. Men are the boss.'

. Nilles, speaking of the Chimbu in the area between Kundiawa and Kerowagi, says (1950:48):

> The women's sex as such is considered by men as dan-gerous; and the woman as a person, because of her sex, is thought mentally inferior to men. Menstru-ation blood is regarded as highly infectious to man but not to woman.

Even the sight of menstrual blood in a river could make a man ill, according to Nilles.

Nilles (1950:47), again referring to the 'Chimbu proper', claims that sexual intercourse before or outside marriage is contrary to the social code. He claims (1950:30) that 'the family ordinarily represents a strong biological unit' (empha-sis mine), and that promiscuity (until the 1950s) was prac-

tically unknown 'even during the emotional times of great
festivities'. This accords with my informants' more recent
information regarding the Chimbu in this area. In other parts
of the Chimbu it seems likely that extramarital sexual relations might have been entered into more readily.

Sexual services do not appear to be such an integral part
of the marriage relationship as they are in many societies.
Barnett (1970:91-2) cites examples of couples who had been
married for a few months before consummation took place.
This occurred in ten of the fourteen marriages discussed by
Barnett. Of the four cases where it did not occur, one was
a case of wife-stealing, one was a widow marriage, and two
were cases where the couple lived with the bride's family
immediately after the marriage instead of the more customary
residence with the husband's people. However, one husband
who had not consummated his second, polygynous marriage after
three years was publicly berated by his mother.

A wife is expected to give birth and nurture children for
her husband, and sexual intercourse is necessary for this;
but it is a relationship fraught with tension, and may not
be very pleasurable. Sexual intercourse among the Chimbu does
not seem to have the emotional or spiritual overtones that it
has in some other societies. Abstention from intercourse over
considerable periods of time, as dictated by the code of society, is apparently practised by many couples. The pattern of
life, separate houses for men and women, separate activities,
separate interests, fear of pollution by women, fear of harm-
ing one's children,[1] fear of being laughed at by other men,
and possibly the type of diet,[2] may all contribute to such
behaviour. A man gains prestige not from his sexual prowess
and the number of feminine conquests he can make, nor even
from the number of children that his wife bears him, but
rather from his strongmindedness in avoiding too much contact
with the opposite sex. When sexual attachments do occur,
either casual or as a preliminary to a free-choice marriage,
both the man concerned and society at large say that the relationship was initiated by the girl and, as one man put it,
'Men are weak, when a girl shows her interest we cannot
resist', or 'She wanted it, so I married her'. The man tries
to make out that he was a passive, somewhat disinterested
partner in the relationship.[3]

---

[1] See p.31.

[2] See p.31, fn.2.

[3] In the case of a man who had carnal knowledge of his pre-
pubertal daughter, it was accepted without question that the

It is considered disgraceful for a wife to have too many children (more than four or five) and even worse for her to have children less than about four years apart. A husband is expected to abstain from sexual intercourse while his wife is pregnant or breastfeeding and there are many social norms and practices which support this ideology, such as separate houses for husbands and wives, many activities carried out by men in a group without their wives, and little social contact between husband and wife.[1] A married man whose wife is not breastfeeding or pregnant will sometimes sleep at her house for a period of about six months, after which it is expected that she will be pregnant, and he will sleep in the men's house. Older men berate a young man whose wife becomes pregnant while she is still breastfeeding her previous child: 'Why, are you a dog with no control, to be always associating with your wife?'

Chimbu believe that having intercourse with a lactating woman will put poison into her milk, making the child ill or causing death. Some also believe that if a man has intercourse with another woman when his wife is breastfeeding, the child will be adversely affected. Chimbu fathers are very fond of their small children and a man is expected to think of them and forego sexual intercourse for the time being.[2]

If wives discover that their husbands have had relations with other women they will be angry but will not regard it as a very serious offence. It would certainly be considered better for a man to have sexual intercourse with another woman than to have intercourse with his wife when she is pregnant or breastfeeding.

---

3 (cont'd)
girl initiated the relationship, and there was no sympathy for the girl, only for the mother; the father was not condemned by his own social group but was by his wife's, who traditionally would have killed him.

[1] Kiki and Beier (1969:16-19) describe a similar system existing among the Orokolo of the Papuan Gulf before the arrival of European missionaries. A woman who is seen to be always with her husband is considered to be the type of wife who will readily be attracted to other men. It is not considered good for a wife to want to follow her husband everywhere 'like a dog'.

[2] The Chimbu diet is very low in protein, particularly animal protein, and fat (Bailey and Whiteman 1963). Some nutrition research indicates that an inadequate diet may lead to decreased libido (Keys et al. 1950:839-40).

When co-wives quarrel it is usually over material goods and does not appear to be because of sexual or emotional jealousy. When a wife becomes angry because, for example, her husband and his agnates have built a new house for the other wife and not for her, it may not simply be that she is angry because she does not have a new house or because her pride is hurt, but she may also be jealous because she regards this as an indication that her husband likes the other wife more than her. However, given the very strong economic motivation that is characteristic of Chimbu and the fact that marriage partners are not regarded as important sources of emotional satisfaction, the feeling of economic deprivation, and jealousy arising from it, is likely to be a stronger element in her anger than a sense of emotional deprivation.

Chimbu men and women are well aware that women who have children in quick succession become thin, tire easily and find it hard to look after two or more young children as well as do their regular work. The low protein diet may be a factor in this. For some women the process of child-bearing is painful. Consequently women themselves do not want children in quick succession and may therefore discourage the sexual interest of their husbands. Some Chimbu claim that there are herbs women can use to prevent conception, but these are usually said to permanently prevent a woman from conceiving. I suspect that these tales have come about more as a means of explaining why some women are barren rather than as a result of their positive use in order to prevent additional pregnancies.

In addition to the specific social attitudes and practices already discussed in relation to male-female relations, several social factors deter acts contrary to the norms of society. These help to reduce discrepancies between the ideology of society and the behaviour of individuals in the sphere of male-female relationships, as well as in other spheres of life.

One informant in Port Moresby mentioned fear of starting fights between groups of agnates as a reason for men avoiding premarital and extramarital love affairs in the time before pacification. Lack of privacy, and gossip can also constrain a person's behaviour. In the Chimbu men are living and working in a closely knit group of kinsmen; there are no newspapers, radios or books so that talking about other people and their activities is an important pastime. It is difficult for a man's actions to pass unnoticed and this acts as a form of social control, as a man depends upon his group in so many respects.

The Chimbu believe that their land is full of witches and
other evil spirits. If a man offends a relative by, for
example, showing too much interest in his relative's wife,
then the relative might harm him or one of his children
through the agency of his supernatural powers. If a wife
does not give food to her husband's siblings, they might become angry and harm her, if they are possessed by supernatural powers. As it is not always known who has supernatural
powers it is best not to offend anyone as far as this is possible.

Children

Children belong to their father, and through him to their
father's subclan and clan. People believe that the father
alone is responsible for conception, and the wife merely looks
after the children, both in utero and after. Child care,
particularly for boys, seems to be almost as much a group as
a parental activity, but ultimate responsibility for children
still lies with the father.

Fathers take great interest in their children when they
are young although their mothers look after them (which involves very little), under the direction of their husbands.
It is a common sight in the Chimbu to see a rugged, weather-
beaten man, his face all smiles, playing with his small son
or daughter on his knee or in his arms. Men want children,
and they get angry with wives who do not bear them any, thinking they do so deliberately. Men want sons to help them work
their land and to inherit from them. They want daughters to
exchange, usually indirectly, for wives for their sons, and
to help their own wives produce food and do other work. Women
want children as a source and object of love and affection.
They want daughters to help them garden, carry water and firewood, look after the pigs, and later to obtain brideprice for
them. They want sons who will look after their rights and
interests when their own brothers have died or are too old.
And everyone wants people to add to their own social group,
for it is the kin group rather than the individual that is
important in Chimbu ethic.

Boys, and girls up to the age of about seven years, may
sleep in the men's house with their father, or spend time
there once they are weaned. As the boys grow older their
fathers and close kinsmen teach them many things. Mothers
have little to say about the upbringing of their sons after
they have reached the age of about five years: they simply
provide food for them. Fathers may see little of their daughters after they are about ten years old but nevertheless

maintain ultimate control over them. Although the life of
boys and girls, brothers and sisters, becomes segregated at
an early age, this does not mean that there are no social or
emotional ties between brothers and sisters. Adult brothers
have an important role to play in guarding the interests of
their sisters, and, if a woman's father is dead, her brother
will come to her aid in any disagreement with her husband or
her husband's kin. Ties between first cousins of different
sexes are similar to those between brother and sister and are
usually expressed in the same terms.[1]

Daughters learn from their mothers, grandmothers and other
female relatives by simply being with them and joining in
their activities. If they do something incorrectly they may
be chastised. Grandmothers, rather than mothers, give girls
simple instructions on manners and behaviour. Girls' puberty
rites are still observed and are joyous occasions.[2] Once a
girl reaches puberty she spends little time helping her
mother by carrying water, looking after younger children or
working in the garden. She no longer regularly fetches pigs
from the garden, nor watches and helps female relatives make
yarn or crochet string bags. Instead she spends her time
with another girl or perhaps two girls, of the same age, wandering about from place to place. These girls wear feathers,
shine their skins with pigs' grease and become plump and
attractive. They enjoy themselves in the various socially
approved activities with young men and married men, sometimes
chaperoned by their female relatives. It is a time of fun
and pleasure, with little responsibility or work to do. For
her parents and their kin groups, the onset of puberty indicates that in due course they will be able to collect brideprice for her. Once a girl is married, or is planning to
marry, she has to work hard for her in-laws or her antici-
pated in-laws; her pattern of life changes drastically.

Sons spend most of the day with the sons of other men of
their father's men's house, catapulting birds, searching for
edible insects, learning to use a bow and arrow, spinning
tops made from the fruit of a tree, or playing other boys'
games. They play in groups and learn from each other as well
as from their fathers and adult kinsmen. At night they listen

---

[1] This close relationship does not seem to exist between
children of the same father but of different mothers.

[2] For descriptions of traditional Chimbu puberty rites for
girls see Ross (1965) and Whiteman (1965).

Plate 5. A girl emerging from confinement at the conclusion of her puberty ceremony.

to the men in the men's house discussing disputes, ceremonial activities, pigs, women and witchcraft.

Boys' initiation ceremonies seem to have been one of the first Chimbu traditional ceremonies to die out. Today young men have plenty of time to sit around talking, gambling and, since 1963, drinking with older men. They also visit various kinsmen and kinswomen, either alone or with other young men. With pacification they are able to wander further afield than in the past, and may develop various relationships with single teenage girls over a wide area. During these wanderings they are gladly housed and fed by their kinsfolk.

Children only belong to their father if he, or his subclan section, has paid brideprice for the mother. If brideprice has not been paid, the children belong to their mother and her social group. However, traditionally the latter rarely occurred because if a couple eloped and tried to live openly together, the woman's kinsmen would demand payment for her or take her back home.

If a single girl becomes pregnant from a casual relationship, she will name a man whom she likes as the father.[1] His
kinsmen will try to persuade him to marry her either in order
to avoid a fight with the girl's kin, or because they think
she would make a suitable bride for him.

External and internal
family relationships

The traditional Chimbu family is an economic and child-
producing unit. It is linked through the husband to the social,
political and economic exchange units of his subclan and tribe.
It is also a link between the husband's subclan section and
the wife's natal kin group.[2]

The traditional Chimbu family has two distant sets of external social relationships: (i) the family as a unit is
politically, economically and socially part of the husband's
agnatic group; (ii) the husband and wife are a link in an
economic exchange and social system between the husband's
subclan section and the wife's subclan section of birth. In
both these sets of relationships the husband is the active
element, the wife the passive element. Her activities are
performed on an individual basis, either directly, in her
relationships with her own natal group, or indirectly, through
her husband, in her activities concerned with her husband's
kin group. It is the husband who lives and acts directly as
a member of a corporate group, spending much of his time in
group activities which serve both individual and group interests. His wife supports him in these by providing food,
children and other services.

Within the family there is strict segregation and specialisation of roles, this segregation being more marked in the
western than in the eastern Chimbu. There are almost no
joint conjugal activities, and husband and wife spend very
little of their time together. A good husband is one who
works hard and gives presents to his affines. Whether his
diligence can be interpreted as a demonstration of affection
for his wife I cannot say. A good wife is one who works hard,
and in particular looks after her own and her husband's pigs;
she does what she is told by her husband and his agnatic kin;

---

[1] This situation was more likely to occur in the eastern part
of Chimbu, as sanctions against premarital sexual relations
were not so strong there as in the west.

[2] See pp.25-6.

she bears her husband's children and looks after them under
his direction; she entertains his visitors without complaint.
Husbands live communal lives with the other men in the men's
house. Women live more isolated lives in their individual
houses.

A strong segregation of the sexes does not necessarily mean
that women are completely subjugated to men. It may mean that
within their own spheres of interest each sex is in control of
its own affairs. However, frequently in affairs of overall
interest, such as politics and introduced economic activities,
men dominate. Such a social arrangement exists in Chimbu.[1]
In societies where there is a closer relationship between men
and women, where husbands and wives frequently work together,
it may be that men dominate in all spheres, or it may be that
there is frequent consultation and companionship between the
spouses.

Sexual and emotional satisfaction seem to be of little
importance in the marriage relationship, which would be con-
sistent with the attitude of Chimbu men that women are a potential source of danger and pollution. However, in spite of
this and the rigid division of labour between the sexes, there
are opportunities for a husband and wife to help each other.
A husband may chop firewood for his wife or carry water for
her, although the latter is considered to be woman's work. A
woman may help her husband by carrying bundles of kunai grass
for him when he is building a house. Such actions are not
demanded by society but are performed voluntarily, according
to the choice of individuals. Possibly they could be interpreted as actions expressing love and affection for one's
spouse. Langness (1969:47) suggests that for the Bena Bena,
to the east of Goroka:

> ...despite the ethos of male superiority and the
> absence of romantic love, strong bonds of affec-
> tion can develop...over the years out of respect
> for one another's labour and skills, shared

---

[1] In 1972 an educated Chimbu wife who had just spent six
months in Chimbu said that in regard to coffee production, the
women were just like labourers, and did not get a fair deal
from their husbands. She also noted that women were beginning to come together in groups and to formulate attitudes on
a group basis. In 1961-62 women in Gumine could not form a
pressure group to influence or oppose men. If they are able
to in the future, it is likely to be part of a radical change
in the relationship between men and women in Chimbu society.

experiences, and common endeavours. Husband and
wife constitute a team, and both gain in status
and prestige.

Chapter 3

Conjugal segregation and social networks
of London and rural Chimbu families

The London families

Bott (1971) describes the exploratory study that she, a
social anthropologist, together with two psycho-analysts and
a social psychologist, made of twenty London families. From
the data collected, Bott developed the hypothesis (1971:60)
that 'the degree of segregation in the role-relationship of
husband and wife varies directly with the connectedness of
the family's social network'. By 'the connectedness of the
family's social network' Bott means 'the extent to which the
people known by a family know and meet one another independently of the family' (Bott 1971:59). Bott uses the terms
'close-knit' to describe a network where a large number of
social relationships between persons in the family's social
network existed independently of the family itself, and
'loose-knit' to describe a network where there are few such
independent relationships between the people forming a family's
social network.

The main emphasis of Bott's study was on internal family
relationships, and in particular on the husband-wife role-
relationship, analysed in terms of the degree of segregation
or jointness in the organisation of their activities. Activities were classified as being of one of three types (Bott 1971:
53):

Complementary organisation -'activities of the husband
and wife [that] are different and separate but fitted
together to form a whole'.

Independent organisation - 'activities [that] are
carried out separately by husband and wife, without
reference to each other, in so far as this is possible'.

Joint organisation - 'activities [that] are carried
out by husband and wife together, or the same activity
carried out by either partner at different times'.

All three types of activity organisation occurred in all the families Bott studied, but their proportions varied in the different families. It was on the basis of the differing proportions of complementary and independent activities in relation to the proportion of joint activities that the conjugal role-relationship of husband and wife was described as being segregated, intermediate or joint. Unfortunately Bott does not say what these proportions were.

Other researchers have used different criteria to evaluate the degree of segregation in the conjugal relationship.[1] In my study of urban Chimbu families I have attempted to use the same criteria as Bott, although due to differences in the ways of life of Chimbu and London families this presented some difficulties, particularly in connection with quantitative analysis.

On the basis of the degree of connectedness in the social networks of the families studied and the degree of segregation in the husband-wife relationship, Bott (1971:61-2) classified the families into four types:

(i) Those with a highly segregated conjugal role-relationship associated with a close-knit social network.

(ii) Those with a joint conjugal role-relationship associated with a loose-knit social network.

(iii) Those with an intermediate degree of conjugal segregation associated with a medium-knit social network.

(iv) Transitional families, that is families that were changing from one type of social network to another, but had not fully adapted to their new situation.[2]

Rural Chimbu families

The husband-wife relationship of the traditional Chimbu family is highly segregated. There are very few joint

---

[1] See Bar-Yosef (1970), Harrall-Bond (1969), Mogey (1956), Blood and Wolfe (1960), Turner (1967).

[2] Two other possible combinations of conjugal role-relationship and social network, i.e., a highly segregated husband-wife relationship and a loose-knit social network, or a joint conjugal relationship and a close-knit social network, were not found among the families studied by Bott (1971:62).

activities and a high proportion of both complementary and
independent activities.[1] Those joint activities that there
are, are usually performed on the basis of personal choice,
as an expression of assistance rather than a norm for the
organisation of a particular activity. This would probably
be true for some joint activities of the London families, but
not for all of them.[2]

For the purpose of economic production the Chimbu family
is a unit in its own right, although it may be dependent upon
clan or other group membership for access to land. In terms
of economic distribution and consumption the family functions
less as a separate unit and more as an integral part of a
large kin group. In terms of social and political relationships the family and the husband-wife relationship are to a
very high degree encapsulated within the husband's kin group,
while each spouse's emotional ties tend to be with their respective natal groups.

A family's social network consists of the husband's kin
group and the wife's kin group. Each of these kin groups is
very closely knit within itself, but their relationship with
each other is in most cases dependent upon the marriage union
of one, or two, couples.[3] As mentioned, the husband is the
active element in such linkages, but the wife has an important, although more passive, role to play. The performance of
specific social, economic and sometimes political activities
by both husband and wife is necessary to maintain relationships between the groups.

The kin groups of husband and wife are linked in a similar
manner, through affinal links, to other groups. Ideally there
are two marriage links between each kin group because if a
woman is married into one group it is expected that in time
a woman of the receiving group will marry into the donor's
group. However, it is considered undesirable to have a large
number of affinal links between the same two kin groups as
each kin group wants to have affinal ties, which are social,
political and economic in nature, with as many outside groups
as possible (Brown 1964:1).

A wife has few social relationships outside her own natal
group and her husband's kin group. The husband, however, may

---

[1] See Appendix B.

[2] For example, joint recreational activities are not an
expression of mutual help.

[3] See pp.25-6, 36.

have a close friendship with an age-mate, and a number of
trading relationships with men in outside groups. This type
of family social network is similar in some respects to that
of the London family studied by Bott where the conjugal role-
relationship was segregated and the social network closely
knit. In this family husband and wife tended to have separate
social networks although sometimes the wife was friendly with
the wives of her husband's friends. Social relationships outside the kin group tended to be sex-segregated, the wife having women friends and the husband men friends. Kin relationships were more important in this London family than they
were in those families with a joint conjugal role-relationship,
particularly for the wife. The husband was not so involved
with kin, and his friends tended to be work-mates who were
also neighbours and who might have similar political interests
to himself. The main difference between this family's social
network and that of the rural Chimbu is that for the latter
the marriage link does not act as a link between two closely
knit groups of people although it does link each spouse to
the natal family of the other spouse. Also there are not so
many occasions when the London family acts as a unit either
within the domestic sphere or in relationships with people
or groups outside of the family. For the Chimbu, where the
wife becomes to a considerable extent a social, political and
economic member of her husband's kin group, the husband and
wife frequently function as a single unit even though their
activities are performed on a segregated basis. In the domestic and economic production spheres the activities of husband
and wife are highly segregated; in their external social relationships they function very much as a joint unit, encapsulated within the kin group of the husband,[1] although the
activities involved in these relationships are performed by
the husband and wife separately. A wife is expected to provide food for her husband's friends, age-mates or trading
partners when they visit him, but she is not expected to have
independent social contact with these friends or their wives.

---

[1] An important basis for this is the payment of brideprice
by the husband and his kinsmen. This entitles them to services
from the woman, since a husband regards his wife as part of
his property.

Chapter 4

Social categories

Status and class in Chimbu society

Traditional Chimbu society was characteristically egalitarian, and everyone lived very much the same way regardless of
status. Status was achieved, not ascribed, and a man gained
status according to what he could give to the group. Chimbu
leaders were usually men who had initially established themselves as fight leaders. In return for gifts of wives, pigs
or land they gave good leadership and made large presentations
of food and valuables at the various gift-exchanges. However,
if the followers considered that a leader was no longer providing good leadership, they simply changed their allegiance
to another man.

Chimbu still tend to respect individuals rather than roles,
and in a society strongly orientated towards reciprocal exchange they respect those individuals who, in their eyes, contribute most to the good of their social group. In the past,
Western society, with its tradition of ascribed positions of
power and prestige, tended to give status to roles rather
than to individuals. However, with rapid social change and
the development of individualism in the twentieth century, a
trend seems to have developed in Western society to give
status to achieved roles, and to the individuals who occupy
these roles, as well as to traditional, high-status, ascribed
roles. In most societies people who occupy high-status positions are expected to live and behave in a manner somewhat
distinct from that of the rest of society. People who achieve
high status frequently try to emulate this way of life, the
upper class way of life, and prestige is given to the way of
life itself. The terms upper, middle and lower class are in
part terms relating to status within a society, but they also
refer to different life-styles. They are classifications
accepted by society as a whole. There seem to have been no
parallels to these social classes in the highlands of Papua
New Guinea.

In Port Moresby expatriates and most well-educated Papua
New Guineans accord high status to educated, Western-orientated
Chimbu, and low status to uneducated, low-income-level Chimbu
who live a more traditional way of life. They classify them
on the basis of socio-economic level and life-style,[1] in much
the same way that social status is viewed in Western society.
In contrast, the Chimbu themselves, whether living in town or
in Chimbu, excepting perhaps the most highly educated, do not
give status in terms of education or occupation but in terms
of what people are doing for their social group. Income level,
of itself, does not earn prestige but generosity, with gifts
of money, food or other valuables, does.

The average uneducated Chimbu in Port Moresby feels sus-
picious of well-educated Chimbu, except for those to whom he
is closely related and knows well. Their way of life is very
different to his own, and they have many contacts with non-
Chimbu, including expatriates. They do not play an active
part in his life and he feels they do not understand him and
his problems. He does not necessarily give respect and high
status to these people simply because they are educated or
have more money than he has. He gives status to people he
knows, people he is in direct contact with, and whom he believes are helping or trying to help him with his needs and
problems, people who understand him.

Politicians, provided they communicate with and listen to
the people, are likely to be given high status whatever their
education. This is because Chimbu see the politicians' work
as being to help them to obtain the things which they want.
A school-teacher might concentrate all his efforts on teaching in the classroom, and be an excellent teacher, but if he
spends his free time with other teachers or in studying it is
unlikely that he will be given a high status in the community
because the people cannot see what he is doing for them. In
contrast, a husband in my sample, who had had no formal education, spoke no English and was not a Christian, was highly
respected as a 'father' and leader by many Chimbu in Port
Moresby. This was because he went among them, particularly
the men from his sub-district, talking with them, listening
to their problems and giving advice, as well as socialising
with them. He was generous in giving money and accommodation
to his relatives, although he had a large family to support
on a low wage. Many kinsmen lived in his house, most of them

---

[1] Education level is often but not always an important factor
related to the socio-economic status of Papua New Guineans.

contributing little or nothing towards the cost of food, rent or power.[1] Occasionally he organised traditional activities among the people of his social group. He was a hard, reliable worker and got on well with expatriates because of these traits, and because of his pleasing personality. He could speak for his group or for individuals when they needed to deal with expatriates.

The three social categories used in this analysis of urban Chimbu families are based on expatriate rather than Chimbu concepts. I use them as a technique for analysing results and comparing findings in different types of family, and as a means of simplification and comparison. In contra-distinction to Bott (1971:62) who grouped her families only after she had assessed her results, because she was not interested in try- ing to include all strata of society in her sample, I grouped my families as I was gathering my sample.

The categories seem similar to social classes in some res- pects, as they are based largely upon the life-style of the families, but they bear little relationship to social status within the Chimbu community in Port Moresby. They are not social classifications which the Chimbu themselves would re- cognise. They are based on a subjective interpretation of life-style and for this reason I call them social categories rather than social classes.

After a preliminary subjective analysis of life-styles I classified the families as falling into one of three cate- gories: unsophisticated (category I), semi-sophisticated (category II), and sophisticated (category III). Categories I and II were much more similar in their life-styles and attitudes than were categories II and III.

Method of categorisation

An attempt was made to correlate my subjective assessment with some objective criteria which it was considered might affect the families' patterns of living and which are usually associated with social class in Western society. With the exception of social category III families, I did not find close correlations with the factors considered. The two factors which gave the closest agreement were educational

---

[1] Brown (1972:41, 93) comments that in the Chimbu a powerful man usually has a group of dependants who form part of the men's house group. These men provide services for their leader in return for past help.

level[1] of the wife and the combined educational levels of
husband and wife. Neither income nor length of stay in Port
Moresby of husband or wife agreed well with type of life-style.
However, where husband and wife both had comparatively high
levels of education, the families were all in category III.
A high education level enabled either husband or wife to earn
comparatively high salaries, which in turn enabled them to
live in a more sophisticated style than otherwise. But income of itself did not put people into category III for there
were families with higher incomes than all or some of the
category III families in both categories I and II (see Table
4.1).

Another factor which may have influenced the life-style of
the families was their relationship with kin, particularly
with kin living in Port Moresby. This relationship would, in
turn, be affected to some extent by the couple's education
and income.

Chimbu living in Port Moresby may be dependent upon kin
for financial reasons, emotional reasons, including a feeling
of duty towards them, or for physical protection. In all
these dependency relationships there is an understood reciprocal obligation to give, when one has something to give, to
those who are in need.[2] This reciprocity is reinforced by
traditional factors, such as fear of witchcraft against a
person who does not fulfil his traditional kinship obligations,
and the fact that when Chimbu go home, as most intend to do,

_____

[1] I refer to secular education only. In the past some missions
trained village people in Bible studies, and reading and writing in vernaculars. These people were expected to give simple
Christian leadership and instruction to others in their villages. They were not trained for paid employment and only
changed their way of life in regard to practices considered
incompatible with Christianity. Three husbands in the sample
had received this type of education, but it did not notice-
ably affect their home life in Port Moresby. In fact,
religion did not seem to be a factor in determining Chimbu
family relationships, apart from its effect upon polygyny.

[2] Chimbu in unskilled employment, like many other Papua New
Guineans, frequently lose their jobs, usually for reasons that
they do not fully understand. There is no stigma attached to
being dismissed, but it may be some time before a man can find
another job. During this time he relies on his kinsmen and
clansmen for support but in a few weeks or months, when he
has found a job, he may be supporting some of them.

they may need help from kin there. Most Chimbu also consider
it to be Christian to help fellow Chimbu.

The number of kin living in Port Moresby will affect the
degree of influence that kin may have on the life of the
families. Several husbands and/or wives regularly sent home
money to parents or brothers in Chimbu, but it is those kin
living in Port Moresby for long periods of time, who have the
greatest effect. Some people live with others without contributing financially to household expenses and have an
'unsophisticating' effect upon the family. Close relationships with kin form a force that pulls against social change
and tends to preserve traditional customs.

Table 4.1 sets out the families in social categories, as
subjectively assessed according to their life-style, against
the education of the wife, the combined educational levels of
husband and wife, and the total family income. In only two
families, P and R, was anyone other than the husband or wife
contributing more than a dollar a week to household finances.
Table 4.1 does not include information relating to kin ties,
due to the difficulty of presenting qualitative information
in tabular form and quantitative information alone would be
misleading in the context of the table.

Category I contains 13 of the 20 families, in only 4 of
which had either husband or wife received any formal education.[1]

Category II is a heterogeneous collection of families that
were transitional or intermediary in their way of living.
Only family N was intermediary in its educational level, but
income levels were in the middle range. It was, however,
difficult to estimate the income of these families due to
fortnightly variations in overtime pay. Their life-style was
more similar to that of category I families than that of
category III, and they could justifiably be considered a sub-
section of category I.

Category III contains only three families, in all of which
the husband had received a secondary education. The wives
had all received a full primary education, and two had had
secondary and some tertiary training. All the husbands and

---

[1] If family G had been able to find better accommodation they
might have fitted into category II, although the husband felt
very strongly that despite his low income it was his Christian
duty to care for the young, single men in Port Moresby from
his village area. This resulted in an unsophisticated type
of living for the family.

Table 4.1

Social category, secular education and income
levels of twenty Chimbu families in Port Moresby

Family	Social category	Education of wife (years)	Combined education of husband and wife (years)	Approximate household income per fortnight ($)
A	I	0	0	34
B	I	0	0	38*
C	I	0	0	20
D	I	0	0	10 + overtime**
E	I	0	0	25
F	I	0	3	60* + overtime**
G	I	3	3	-***
H	I	0	0	20
I	I	0	0	14
J	I	0	0	53*
K	I	0	3	200*
L	I	0	0	34
M	I	0	9	84
N	II	1	5	25 + overtime**
O	II	0	0	40
P	II	0	0	40≠ + overtime**
Q	II	0	3	-*** + overtime**
R	III	6	15 +	88≠
S	III	9#	19 +	48*
T	III	7#	13 +	90

*   Includes income earned by wife.
** Varies each fortnight.
*** Income too irregular to assess.
≠   Includes income earned by other members of the household.
Plus tertiary education after one or more years of high
    school.

two of the wives had been to boarding school. The income
levels of these families were comparatively high, but were
not the highest of all the families. There were only three
sophisticated families in the sample because there were very
few such Chimbu families at the time of my study. I found
only five in Port Moresby; in one of these there were marital
problems and the wife and children went back to Chimbu to live
during my survey. I omitted the other family in order to
maintain the anonymity of the category III families, and be-

cause I had not included all possible families in the less
sophisticated classifications.

Table 4.1 does not indicate a strong agreement between
life-style, education and income, except possibly in category
III, where there was an overall relationship between life-
style and education. This relationship was modified by relationships with kin and by income levels, which in themselves
might be affected by education. If a man did not have a sufficiently large income his family would not be able to live
in the manner characteristic of families in category III. If
a family had high income but not an adequate level of education, it would not have the concepts to motivate it to live
in the style of category III families.

Religion

Religion was not found to be a significant factor in determining the life-styles of the families. There were pagans,
Catholics and Lutherans in social categories I and II including some active church members and some who had given up practising Christianity. In social category III there was one
disinterested Catholic, the rest of the spouses being Lutherans.

Geographical mobility

The families studied were all geographically mobile in the
sense that they were not living in the Chimbu, where the husband and wives were born, lived and were socialised.[1] Some
of the couples married and lived as families in the Chimbu,
others had lived as a family only in Port Moresby. Bott (1971:
106-8) considers that when families move away from the neighbourhood where the husband and wife have been living for all
or most of their lives, their social network will become less
tightly knit, especially if previously the family had a close-
knit social network. This situation may be modified for the
Chimbu families because so many of their kinfolk had also
come to live in Port Moresby. It was almost as if a part of
a closely knit neighbourhood had moved, rather than an individual family.

The social category I and II families were mobile within
Port Moresby and many of them also left the city. During the
study, 4 of the 17 families in these categories changed their
residence. Between late 1971 and August 1973, 8 of these

---

[1] Two exceptions have been noted (see p.7). On the socialisation of some category III spouses, see p.80.

families had moved their residence within the city and 4 had
left Port Moresby; one other family had moved within Port
Moresby before finally leaving the city. Many of their neighbours and kin were equally mobile. The social category III
families did not move during the study, but two families had
since left Port Moresby.

Chapter 5

Social category I families

Introduction

The attitudes and practices of the unsophisticated families
were probably the closest to traditional Chimbu attitudes and
behaviour. Most families in my sample fell into this category,
as would the majority of Chimbu families living in Port Moresby
at the time of writing (1973). Most husbands and wives had no
formal education although a few had had some simple mission
training.[1]

Six of the thirteen families lived in shanty towns in
houses that they or their relatives had built from pieces of
scrap wood and scrap-metal sheeting. There was no piped water,
no drainage and no electricity. Most homes had no furniture
apart from a home-made wooden bed-cum-bench and a wooden box
with a padlock for valued possessions. Cooking was done outside, over an open fire. Most families lived in one room,
which they often had to share with their kinsmen, and much of
the everyday living was carried on outside, sitting on mats,
the bare ground, or in a doorway.

Two of the families formed part of a compound household
with another married couple and a number of single men or boys.
Sometimes all the single boys slept in one or other of the two
very small rooms meant for them. At other times there were
too many of them and one or two slept in the same room as
their married kinsman and his family. During my study only
one husband in my sample of families living in a shanty settlement was unemployed, but several single men who lived with
them had been without work for months, and were fed by those
who did have work.

Domestic life

Only one meal was eaten daily, usually boiled rice with
tinned meat or tinned fish. Three wives had jobs, but for the

---

[1] See p.46, fn.1.

Plate 6. Houses in a shanty settlement. On the left is a small, family-type house and on the right is a long dormitory for single men.

Plate 7. A low-covenant house. Such houses are frequently inhabited by about fifteen people.

others, after sweeping out the house, which took about five minutes each day, and washing a few cotton clothes, which took about half an hour a day, there was very little for them to do. As the need arose, and if they had any money, they walked to the nearest tradestore to buy rice or a tin of fish or meat, or a packet of tea or sugar. Gambling was popular, and if a woman did not have money herself, she whiled away the hours watching others play.

Most of the husbands did manual work and were tired when they came home. They sat around for half an hour, ate, and when it became dark they went to sleep. At the weekends, if it was 'pay' fortnight, they spent most of the time, day and night, drinking or gambling; on the alternate weekend they usually looked for kinsmen or other Chimbu with money to buy them drinks, or watched gambling. Sometimes kinsmen visited them. Some went to church on Sundays, but others had no money for the bus fare and found it too hot to walk in the sun, especially if they had young children.

This life-style was similar for all category I families, whether living in shanty settlements, in a low-cost self-help housing settlement, in a low-cost housing suburb or in an institutional house. However, in the latter the institution usually had regulations prohibiting anyone but their employee's immediate family living with him, and permission had to be gained in advance for an overnight guest. The three families living in a low-cost self-help housing settlement formed a compound household, they and four young single men living in one-and-a-half rooms of a three-room house. The other one-and-a-half rooms were occupied by two families and a single teenage boy from the Eastern Highlands.

Chimbu women did not like being left by themselves in Port Moresby, although in Chimbu they live in houses on their own with their children. Boredom was one reason; another was that they felt very nervous with so many strangers around them. They said there were many murders in the city. One woman went to her husband's work-place and waited under a tree all day with their two-year-old child. Another had her husband's unemployed kinsmen to keep her company at home, and those living in compound households had the other women of the household with them.

Wives in the compound households usually cooked at the same time, but each bought (if she had the money) her own food and provided some for each meal. Sometimes each woman cooked in an individual saucepan, sometimes the food was cooked in the one saucepan; either way the food was dished up together and

Plate 8.   Card-playing is an important recreation in
shanty settlements.

shared between the families and any single men and boys present. This was similar to the system in the Chimbu where each
day a wife collects and cooks her own sweet potatoes and
green leaves and then shares them with all who are present
at the time. If her husband is not at her house she sends
some cooked food to the men's house for him, where he will
share it with his kinsmen. On one occasion I saw a woman in
Port Moresby parcelling up cooked food to send to an unmarried kinsman in the city. She told me that she did this
regularly.

In Port Moresby, as in Chimbu, food was given to the single
men regardless of whether they had made any direct contribution, financial or otherwise, to the household. Most families in social category I appeared to accept this without complaint. One wife did tell me that her husband sometimes became angry with those who were working but never contributed

to the family budget, but they continued to feed them 'because
my husband is a Christian man and says he would be ashamed if
men from his place went around stealing and getting into
trouble!' This seems to be a new rationalisation of the traditional practice of single men being given food as they visit
from house to house, rather than being the practice of a
Christian ethic. One wife, who worked as a domestic servant
during the day, cooked every evening for herself, her husband,
her husband's child by his first wife, and fourteen kinsmen of
her husband who lived in a home-made dormitory near her house.
Traditional beliefs reinforce this practice of feeding kinsmen
because, it is thought, to offend a relative will bring sick-
ness or death to oneself or to a close member of one's family
as a result of witchcraft.

Couple M lived in a small Housing Commission house in a
low-cost housing suburb. Unlike the other category I families,
the husband attended high school for three years and had a
good job and relatively high income. The house was always
full of people who preferred sitting on the floor to using
the two chairs in the house. Some of these people lived permanently at the house, others came to talk to the husband or
wife. Whether this situation arose from the fact that the
wife was not educated, from the personalities of the husband
or wife, or because the husband had political aspirations and
did not want to offend his potential electorate, I find impossible to say. The wife rather than the husband was not
satisfied with their life-style and would have liked some
people to move out of the house, her husband's kinsmen rather
than her own.

Three families lived, when I began my study, in the grounds
of institutions where either the husband or wife worked. One
family moved to a small three-bedroomed house in the same
suburb as family M during my research. These families lived
very much the same way as the other families except that in
the institutional houses they were not allowed to have relatives living with them. When family A was first allocated
a Housing Commission house they planted out a vegetable garden, collected a few pieces of furniture, and the children
decorated 'their' bedrooms with pictures that they brought
home from school. In fact, the bedrooms were never theirs
because many relatives had moved into the house even before
the family itself moved in.

Children

Relationships with their children reflected one of the most
striking differences between the families in categories I and

Plate 9. Part of a compound household in a shanty settlement.

Plate 10. Wives coming to Port Moresby find they must adapt to new forms of domestic life.

II and those in category III. Parents in category I apparently saw their parental duties as simply feeding and clothing
their children and providing some physical protection. In
town they mostly employed the traditional approach to bringing up children, for they knew no other way. Some wives took
their babies to infant welfare clinics regularly, others only
when they were sick. Parents left many decisions for the
children to make themselves. This was particularly the case
in situations for which there was no traditional precedent.
For example, if a child were sick but did not want to go to
the hospital, the mother gave in and did not take the child
to hospital; a little girl did not like having a shower so
she never had one, although the parents thought that she
should have showers.

Parents made little effort to train their children[1] or to
take any part in their lives. Traditionally, children are
educated through participation in activities with adults.
Parents in Port Moresby continued in this pattern, the difference being that in Port Moresby there was little in which the
children could participate with adults. Fathers sat and played with their infant children, but once they could walk and
run about, parents seemed to take very little personal interest in them. Partly as a result of their changed pattern of
life in town, boys could not go to work with their fathers or
take part in their day-to-day activities; mothers had very
little work to do and little to teach their daughters.[2]

Some parents were very keen that their children go to
school but others either were indifferent and had little am-
bition for their children, or they looked at the future in
terms of the past. Some children attended school and learnt
many things about which parents knew nothing, but parents did
not appear to envisage any great change in their relationships
with their children as a result of education. Parents expected that children who had been to school would wish to remain

---

[1] See p.64, fn.2 for the case of one man who did attempt to
discipline his teenage son and found that his wife and her
relatives opposed the idea. After this incident a younger
child ran away, in case his father hit him, and the boy concerned refused to return home.

[2] Some of the new forms of recreation available in the city
might have provided an opportunity for joint parent-child
activities but either the parents were not interested in such
activities or transportation of the whole family to the venue
of these activities was too great a problem.

in the town and live a different life to that of people in
Chimbu or that of their parents. However, apart from thinking that their children would be economically better off than
they themselves, parents did not have any ideas about how
their children's lives would differ from their own; they left
it to the school to prepare their children for the new way of
life.

When they had money families provided their children with
food; if they did not have any money the children either went
without, which was considered bad, or the parents depended
upon relatives to feed them or give them money, which was not
considered bad. Many wives who were not working had little
say in whether there would be money to buy food. They had
little or no control over their husband's gambling and drinking habits, nor over the arrival of visitors who might have
to be fed, thereby using up a fortnight's food allowance in
one or two days.

In category I families a responsible husband was expected
to give his wife two or more dollars (two dollars buys very
little in Port Moresby) a fortnight as food money. Few wives
complained about the share of their husbands' income that they
were given for food, but complained only that their husbands'
pay was low. A number of husbands and wives thought it was
alright for men to gamble but not women: if women gambled
there would be no money for food. Most of the category I husbands gave their wives money for food but did not give them
a personal allowance.[1]

Formal external relationships

About half of the husbands and many of the wives had no
social relationships with people other than Chimbu; many wives
had no social relationships beyond their own or their husband's
kin. One shanty settlement consisted of clusters of three or
four houses or dormitories of people from different parts of
Chimbu, but the people from the different areas had almost no
contact with one another. One woman from near Kundiawa told
me that she was lonely for the company of other women, yet
she did not talk to the four Sinasina women who lived barely
fifty yards away from her house. Even if they could not have
understood each other's dialects, which was unlikely, they
could have spoken to each other in Pidgin.

---

[1] Similarly in category II families. Those in category III
either gave their wives personal, food and child allowances
or the wife was earning for herself.

Two wives regularly took their babies to infant welfare
clinics; another stayed in hospital for a week during the
study. However, the most common activity coming under the
heading of Bott's 'formal external relationships' was going
to church. At church the families rarely mixed or spoke to
people they did not already know, so that the only formal relationships made in this connection were with church officials.
One couple were going to baptismal classes, and had formal
relationships with their expatriate instructor.

Kuman and Kia[1]

This couple had been married for between thirteen and fifteen years. Neither had had any formal education and both
were pagan. Kia, the wife, wanted to join the Catholic church,
and she and her children sometimes went to church in Port
Moresby. For some years Kuman had been thinking about joining the church, but he was a polygynist and was unwilling to
give up either of his wives.

When I visited Chimbu in 1967 Kuman was a local government
councillor. He had had two wives long before this, perhaps
as the leader of a subclan group. He discussed with me the
reasons why he needed two wives: 'I have to do a lot of entertaining, and I must have a woman to cook for me if one wife
is sick, or if she goes away to visit her family. All wives
must visit their families from time to time'.

'But you are a strong man! You could do your own cooking
for a day or two.'

'That's all right for you white people, but we can't just
open a tin and turn on a switch. The firewood has to be collected, and the sweet potatoes, too. Then there is heating
up the hot stones for the earth oven, and arranging the food
in banana leaves. I simply haven't got the time for all that.
So I must have two wives.'

Kuman had seven living children, three by one wife and
four by the other. Four children were in Port Moresby and
three, one of whom he had never seen until he went on leave,
were in Chimbu with Bre, his second wife.[2]

---

[1] To maintain anonymity all names have been changed. This
couple are taken as an example of a category I family.

[2] On his return from leave Kuman left Kia in the Chimbu, because she was not well, and brought Bre and two sons by her
to Port Moresby, together with Kia's three children.

The household. At the beginning of my study Kuman and Kia
lived in a small two-bedroom weatherboard house in the grounds
of the institution where Kuman worked. With them lived their
three children: Mon, a daughter of about eleven years, Bomai,
aged about eight years, and Kumago, about four-and-a-half
years. Kaupa, Kuman's twelve-year-old son by Bre, also lived
with them.

The house had running cold water, a shower, washtubs,
drains and electric power (although the latter had not been
working for many months). This house, with its facilities,
was of a higher standard than most houses lived in by category I families. Most of the plain, rough furniture belonged
to the institution, but Kuman owned a few cupboards and odd
items given to him by staff at the institution. Outside there
were some large shade trees, and plenty of ground where Kia
had planted pawpaws, beans, corn and sweet potatoes for family
consumption, and peanuts to sell in the market.

No-one except the immediate family lived in the house because the institution forbade relatives other than wife, parents or children to live in an employee's allocated house.
This rule may have caused Kuman to apply for a Housing Commission house, although he never stated this. It certainly
was one of the main reasons why his brother, Die, who worked
and lived at the same institution, applied for a Housing Commission house. Kuman gave me two reasons for applying for
another house: firstly, should he ever lose his job at the
institution he and his family would have nowhere to live;[1]
secondly, he wanted a house for his other wife and their children to live in. Kuman thought that Port Moresby schools were
better than those in Chimbu because children had to speak
English all the time they were at school and not just during
lesson periods. For this reason he wanted his children to be
educated in Port Moresby.[2]

After waiting for over a year, Kuman was allocated a Housing Commission house, but before he and the family had moved
into it three of his relatives from Chimbu arrived in Port
Moresby. They said that they had come because they were angry
with Kuman and Die for not having gone home when their mother
died. These men could not live in the institutional house

---

[1] There was an acute shortage of low-cost housing in Port
Moresby.

[2] Kuman was somewhat unusual in his strong desire to educate
his children. The motivation was economic: they would be able
to get highly paid work when they finished school and give him
money presents.

where Kuman lived, but went to live in the new Housing Commission house, and Kuman decided that he would wait until after he had been on leave to bring Bre and the other children to the city.

Then Kuman was told that he and his family would have to move into the house or it would be reallocated. There was much talking and many tears, but in the end he and his family all moved to the new house except Kaupa, the eldest son, who was just about to take his standard six examinations. He stayed, as a temporary measure, with Kuman's brother and wife, who moved into Kuman's institutional house. Kuman did not want to move, because if they did where would Bre and the other children live? He did not like the long distance and the cost of transport to work each day, and it was difficult to find schools to which the children could transfer. Kia did not want to move because she did not like the garden at the new house and she would be leaving her cultivated garden behind. But move they did.

They had no sooner moved into the small three-bedroomed house, with the three kinsmen still living there, than Kia's father's brother and his son arrived, and they too moved in. They said that they had come because they had heard that Kia was ill, which was true, and that she had died, which was not true. Kuman paid for the rent and rates, the electricity and the food for all these people. One day, when I brought this topic up, one of the kinsmen explained to me: 'In Chimbu when we go to stay with people we don't pay rent or provide food'.

In a situation such as this, with no privacy, it would be difficult for husband and wife to devote much time to each other or to their children. The demands of kin were pressing continuously upon both husband and wife.[1] Kuman made several

---

[1] Recently Kuman, Kia and the children went to Chimbu for six weeks' leave, their fares being paid by Kuman's employer. When they were in Gumine, people whom they had assisted in Port Moresby, or the relatives of these people, gave them plots of garden land to use. Some of the land was in full production and the rest was just coming into production. The land was returned to its original owners when Kuman and family returned to Port Moresby.

In contrast, when couple K returned to Chimbu with the idea of staying there they were not given garden plots and only very little food. This may have been because the husband kept most of the family's large earnings (to buy a second wife) rather than being generous to his own and his wife's kinsmen.

polite suggestions to his kinsmen that they should move out,
but these were ignored. Finally he bought the plane ticket
back to Chimbu for the eldest of the three men, who could
find no work in Port Moresby. Later Kia's uncle left, but
her cousin remained to help look after Kia, who was sick again.
However, Kia's daughter, Mon, did most of the cooking after
she came home from school, boiling rice or root vegetables
with tinned meat or tinned fish. Kuman claimed that he could
not manage without a wife to do the cooking, even in Port
Moresby. Obviously he did not feel that he should help in
domestic tasks, in contrast to his brother, Die, who often
helped his wife with cooking and washing the dishes 'because
she is working for money'.

When Kuman returned from leave three married couples were
living in his house, and he and his wife Bre and the five
children moved in with them. Digini, the ten-year-old son
who had not been in Port Moresby before, was most uncomfort-
able in the crowded conditions and the other children were
not happy. Digini left the house after a week and stayed with
various relatives, occasionally calling in at his father's
home.

Financial arrangements. Kuman's pattern of spending was
interesting. He earned approximately $34 a fortnight net.
After moving to the Housing Commission house he received
about $27 per fortnight net after deductions for rent, garbage
collection, and Public Service Association fees. His electricity bill was about $3.50 a month.

Kuman belonged to a kampani, as did most Chimbu with regular employment. These kampani consist of groups of two or
more people who trust each other, and who each fortnight give
a large portion of their pay to another member, in a rotating
system. When Kuman was living in the institutional house,
where the rent was less, where there was no electricity to
pay for and where relatives could only visit for a few hours
at a time, he belonged to a two-man kampani composed of himself and a work-mate, a man of another tribe. One fortnight
Kuman gave this man $30, the next fortnight the Kerema man
gave him $30. This example of a socio-economic relationship

---

1 (contd)
It may also have been a consequence of social disapproval of
the activities of this couple when in Port Moresby (see p.64
fn.1). After a few weeks the couple returned to Port Moresby
without a second wife, and built a rough timber house in a
shanty settlement.

with a non-Chimbu work-mate was a rather rare occurrence among the families studied. When Kuman moved to Hohola he could no longer manage to give his partner $30 on alternate fortnights, so the kampani broke up. Kuman formed a new one with a Chimbu work-mate, and they each gave or received $20 a fortnight.

The kampani system was very common among Papua New Guineans in the urban centres and apparently arose spontaneously, to meet a felt need to have a little 'capital' in one's pockets from time to time. It does lead, also, to a feast or famine type of existence. Little (1962) reports the existence of similar organisations in West Africa.

Kuman said that under the present arrangements he allocated $5 a fortnight for food. When Kia was well he gave it to her; when she was sick he kept it himself. On the fortnight when he collected from the kampani he gave a dollar or two to each of the children to buy books, school lunches and other things they needed, including their annual school fees. He gave the rest of the money to relatives or used it to gamble. If he won at cards he put money in the bank. If he lost, Kia became angry!!

Like many of the other Chimbu husbands, Kuman did not think that wives should gamble because if they lost there was no money left for food. Husbands in social category I, and most of those in category II, did not give their wives a personal allowance. They only gave them a very small food allowance, as Chimbu resent having to spend money on food. The husbands felt that they were doing the right thing by their wives, even if they did only give them a food allowance. The wife's wish to give presents or money to her relatives was sometimes a source of contention between husband and wife. From the husband's point of view, wives in Port Moresby do very little work, although it is not their own choice to sit around all day. Those who do go out to work are free to spend the money they earn as they like without consulting their husbands.[1]

---

[1] An exception to this was the prostitute (wife K) whose husband handled and controlled all her earnings. Perhaps this was because he always went with her and acted as a go-between, because of the large amount of money involved, or because they decided that the money would be used to buy him another wife to bear him a child, as his present wife, the prostitute, appeared to be barren. But most probably it was because her earnings were regarded as compensation for the husband - for not being given any children, and for forfeiting his sole rights to the sexual services of his wife.

Kuman's life-style. Kuman did not spend much time at home.
He said that Kia accepted this and did not get angry about
it (as we shall see, this may not be strictly accurate), as
some wives would. When he went around the city he played
cards, went to some garden land he had near one of the shanty
settlements, or visited Chimbu relatives or friends. Sometimes he took young Kumago with him, but Kia or the other
children rarely went anywhere with him. He had many friends,
both Chimbu and non-Chimbu, and many kinsmen in Port Moresby.
Most Papuan friends were ones he had made when he was working
in the city previously, just after he married Kia. At this
time there were not many Chimbu in Port Moresby, and, no doubt
because of his pleasing personality, he made many Papuan
friends. Kia had stayed behind in Chimbu but had not borne
him a child. When he returned to Chimbu a year or so later
several young women were keen to marry him. Some came to stay
with his mother for a week or two, but those she did not think
would make good wives were decorated with feathers and sent
back home. Some whom his mother liked, Kia did not like.
Sometimes she fought with them so they ran away. The only
one who remained was Bre, whom both Kia and Kuman's mother
liked.

Kuman had seven living children (one of Bre's children
died), but in contradistinction to traditional views, Kuman
said that he would like more children.[1] He claimed that some
Chimbu men today wanted ten or fifteen children (I never met
any of them!) to send to school and to be trained as doctors
or teachers or for other highly paid work. Then, when their
parents were old, they would have plenty of money to give them.
This example of economic motivation, of Kuman's pragmatic
approach to life, is very characteristic of the Chimbu.

On many occasions Kuman revealed to me his love and respect
for his mother (both he and Die were very proud to be her sons,
and I felt that she was a rather remarkable old lady when I
knew her in Chimbu), but I never saw any signs of affection or
personal interest in Kia or the three older children.[2] As far

---

[1] The traditional Chimbu attitude, as explained in Chapter 2,
is more against having children in rapid succession than
against having a large number of children.

[2] On one occasion Kuman attempted to discipline Kaupa for going against Kuman's wishes. Shortly after, Kaupa went to his
mother's relatives complaining about his father's treatment.
A group of kinsmen came to Kuman's house and began smashing
it up, saying he had been unfair to Kaupa. Such interference
by parents' relatives, which happens frequently, makes it very
difficult for parents to guide their children.

as his daughter was concerned this attitude was traditional, but as regards his sons I feel unable to assess whether this was a traditional attitude, a personality manifestation, or the result of a changed way of life in that boys go to school in Port Moresby to learn things and there is not the same dependency relationship between son and father as there is in Chimbu. However, this type of situation does seem to be characteristic of the father-child relationship among category I and II families. Kuman rarely gave any money or presents to Kaupa, who was now about sixteen years old. He did not understand the needs of an educated urban youth.

Kia's life-style. Kia, a thin, somewhat goitrous-looking woman, had been in hospital once before my study and was admitted again, for a week, during the study. The doctors were unable to find anything wrong with her, and her condition may have been largely psychological, due to general homesickness and worrying about her own parents; the latter state was aggravated by the news of the death of her mother-in-law. During her stays in the hospital, Kuman and many other people visited her. A traditional duty of a husband is to look after his wife when she is sick, and this duty continued in the urban environment.

One day I happened to be present when Kuman came home after visiting people in town. Kia, it seems, had been feeling very ill and wanted to go to hospital. She attacked her husband with a broom and stones, saying that she was ill because he was always going off and leaving her, and that he did not look after her properly. She was restrained, with considerable effort, by two male relatives. Kuman stood and watched, or walked around, saying, 'I am my mother's son. I will not fight. Come, you can fight me, but I will not fight you.... Who paid for your fare to Moresby?'

After this episode Kia spent a week with some of her kinsmen who worked in the same institution as Kuman. The children, Bomai and Mon, went with Kia. Young Kumago and Kaupa stayed with their father. Kia wanted to go back to Chimbu, but this would have meant either leaving the children in Port Moresby or spoiling their chances at school. Kuman said that if Kia went back to Chimbu it was up to the children to decide for themselves whether they wanted to go with her or stop in Port Moresby, but added that Kia could not control Kumago.

If Kia had gone back to Chimbu both Mon and Bomai would probably have gone with her, even though they were both doing well at school. Mon often complained about how her father was never at home and did not give her mother enough money. Kaupa (who was not Kia's son) complained that Kia used to spend the food money his father (Kuman) gave her on buying string to make string bags for her relatives.

Two weeks after the quarrel, Kia cooked a chicken for Kuman and gave him a dollar. I gained the impression that she thought that her behaviour had been un-Christian, and that she was ashamed. This incident indicates some of the things that husband and wives quarrel about: not looking after the sick, not giving the wife enough money, giving too many presents to relatives, wandering around town playing cards rather than staying at home with the family.[1]

Of all the people included in my study, Kia appeared to be the least well adapted to urban life.[2] She had been in Port Moresby for three-and-a-half years but had not learnt to speak Pidgin, as the other wives had done. Kuman found her work as a domestic servant from time to time and taught her how to clean the house or iron clothes, but the jobs never lasted very long. She did not keep her own house clean and tidy or know how to wash cotton clothes properly.

Kia always sat on the floor of the house or on the ground outside rather than on chairs. She said she preferred the traditional system of husbands sleeping in a men's house apart from their wives because 'this was the way my ancestors lived, and the way that I have been taught'. 'But', she said, 'the Moresby way of husbands sleeping in the same room as their wives does not cause any trouble.' She herself wanted one more child, but because she was old and ill and because the children were sleeping in the same room, she was not having sexual relations with her husband. This did not worry her; what did worry her - and the other category I wives who were in a similar position had the same problem - was her complete economic dependence upon her husband. In the Chimbu she was relatively independent of her husband for day-to-day living, but in Port Moresby her small garden was not adequate to supply her family with food, and she had to depend upon her husband to give her money to buy food. This was irritating in itself, but the irritation was aggravated when Kuman went away to his friends to play cards and have a few drinks, leaving her and the children at home without food or money.

---

[1] Strathern (1972:42) reports that among the Melpa near Mt Hagen one of the complaints that a woman may bring against her husband is simply that he does not spend enough time in her company.

[2] None of the wives in category I seemed really happy living in Port Moresby.

The conjugal relationship. The above account indicates
that while Kuman and Kia conducted most of their lives independently and had few shared or joint activities, they were
also dependent upon each other in some respects. Kuman
claimed that he needed a wife in Port Moresby to cook for him
and wash his clothes (and, I would add, to look after his
younger children if he wanted to have them with him in Port
Moresby). Kia was dependent upon Kuman to provide her and
the children with a house and with money for food and clothes,
and to look after her when she was sick. It was a reciprocal
arrangement.

Kuman and Kia did very few things together. Although Kuman
had worked as a domestic servant, he did no domestic work in
his own home, in spite of the fact that it was not kept very
clean. When Kuman went visiting friends Kia stayed at home,
probably as much from her own choice as for other reasons.
There were almost no joint or complementary activities in
their relationship, the only joint activity being when Kuman
taught Kia how to wash and iron clothes so that she could
obtain employment. When she was earning money Kia kept it
herself and used it as she wished.[1]

Bott (1971:53) describes as segregated conjugal relationships those in which there is a low proportion of joint activities. On this basis the conjugal relationship of Kia and Kuman
was highly segregated, with almost all of their activities
being of the independent type. Bott also mentions the sexual
relationship, and the emotional overtones of the conjugal-role
relationship of the couples she studied in addition to the
attitudes and expectations that one partner had towards the
other.

Kuman and Kia had ceased having sexual relations, at least
for the time being. I found no real evidence of an emotional
bond between them, only of Kia's dependency upon her husband.
She had her children with her, but had only a few kinsmen in
Port Moresby as sources of emotional satisfaction. Also she
had very little land on which to garden, and it was not her
own land. Consequently she was homesick. Kuman had many
kinsmen in the city and men from his own part of the Chimbu
whom he met regularly, as well as a number of Papuan friends.
He seemed to obtain considerable emotional satisfaction from
his contacts with all these people, as well as from his
youngest son.

---

[1] Cf. p.14.

Marriage history. I was told that when Kia was about eight
years old her own and Kuman's kinsmen decided that they should
marry when Kia was old enough. This was because one of her
kinsmen had married a kinswoman of Kuman's and, as Kuman put
it, 'We were harvesting what we had planted. Like beans that
grow, produce seeds for new plants and become old and dry, we
were getting new young beans. We were getting a new young
woman to produce children and then grow old'. However, when
Kia saw Kuman and heard stories about how strong he was, she
wanted to marry him. They 'carried leg'[1] and were attracted
to each other.[2]

Social networks. Kuman's social network consisted of a
number of separate sections, each section being closely knit
internally. This was rather different from the social network
types found by Bott in her London families, but similar to
those of traditional Chimbu, as described in Chapter 2.[3] Some
of the sections were organised social groups, the largest and
most important being the kin group. Part of this group was
in Port Moresby and part in the Chimbu. Contact with the
latter was maintained through visitors and letters.

During most of the research period Kuman had the following
kin living in or near Port Moresby, with all of whom he was
in regular contact: one brother (with his wife), two nephews
(one with his wife), six cousins (one of whom had his wife
with him), one maternal uncle, two lineage members and three
clansmen. He was also in contact with most of the Gumine
people in Port Moresby, including his affines. Some of these
men were also his work-mates. Only a few traditional activities such as gift-exchanges were held within this group,[4] and
as far as I know none had been carried out between it and
other social groups. Nevertheless Gumine people in Port

---

[1] Boys and girls sit on the ground with one of the boy's legs
crossed over one of the girl's legs.

[2] Most other arranged marriages in my sample involved a certain amount of persuasion by kinsfolk before the wife was
willing to marry the man they wanted to accept for her. For
one wife it was almost a forced marriage. See Appendix C.

[3] Possibly Kuman's network could be regarded as a transitional
network, in the process of changing from a large, closely knit
network into a loosely knit one, but more details of Kuman's
network and the processes of change in social networks would
be required before such a claim could be substantiated.

[4] When Kuman's eldest daughter reached puberty in 1971 an
attempt was made to have modified puberty rites. Kia was in

Moresby had a feeling of belonging together, of having some
sort of social relationship in common between them, even if
no kin or affinal relationship existed.

The 'Gumine group' was not an organised group to the same
extent that kin groups are organised in the Chimbu for various
types of activity, probably because it did not have many group
activities to perform. It was more like the kin group of the
London family which had a close-knit social network and segregated conjugal relations.[1] Many of the activities within the
'Gumine' group were on an individual-to-individual basis, such
as giving money or food to someone in need. Kuman's main
activities within this group were playing cards and gambling,
listening to news from recent arrivals in Port Moresby about
people in the Chimbu, and settling various disputes between
members.

Kuman's social relationships with other people were mainly
in relation to his work (many of his work-mates were Gumine
men) and with Papuans who trusted him and gambled with him
because they knew that he was not a quarrelsome man.[2] While

---

1 (contd)
the Chimbu when her daughter had her first menstruation.
There was talk of sending the fare for her to return to Port
Moresby in time for the feast which follows the girl's period
of confinement in a house kept warm with fires. As far as I
know, Kia's daughter was the first Gumine girl to have her
puberty rites in Port Moresby although a few months earlier
one had been held for a Gumine girl at Sogeri.

Bre and Kuman's brother's wife and one of the other women
living in the house took it in turns to sit in the hot, stuffy
room with the girl. It was planned to have an all-night singing session such as occurs on these occasions in Chimbu, but
insufficient kinswomen were available in Port Moresby. A number of other ritual activities were also omitted and the period
of confinement was reduced to one week. During this time traditional food tabus were kept. It was fortuitous that menstruation began at the commencement of the school holidays.
Kuman decided that the girl should go back to school for the
new term, against the wishes of his sister-in-law. His daughter was approximately fifteen years old at the time.

1 One important difference was that Gumine people in Port
Moresby were nearly all men.

2 Playing cards without a licence is illegal in Papua New
Guinea. A quarrelsome man might attract attention and cause
the police to investigate the disturbance.

there was a very large economic element in his gambling relationships with Papuans (he saw them as a way of making money),
because of his personality there was also an element of com-
radeship.

Kia had no social relationships outside of Gumine people.
(The only language that she could speak was the Gumine dialect
of Kuman.) She had few kinsfolk in Port Moresby, one niece,
two cousins and one clansman, and recently her uncle and cousin
arrived, having heard that she was ill. Kia was involved to
some extent with Kuman's relatives and friends when they visited
the house, mainly by preparing food for them, but she did not
have close relationships with these people, except perhaps
with the wife of one of Kuman's nephews who came from the same
place as Kia. As we have seen, most of Kuman's kin in Port
Moresby were men; another factor limiting the type of relationship that Kia had with Kuman's kin was that in the Chimbu, traditionally, the wife is a passive link between her own kin
group and that of her husband's group. She is expected to be
hospitable and prepare food for them, but has little direct
contact. Her husband's kin interact directly with her agnatic
kin group. For these reasons I would not regard Kuman and Kia
as having a single social network. When she was living at the
institution where Kuman worked, Kia lived a rather lonely life,
but she seldom, if ever, went to visit the wife of Kuman's
brother who was also living in the grounds of the institution.

In summary, Kuman and Kia had two distinct, but overlapping
social networks in Port Moresby. Kia had a very small network
made up of her kin, who all knew one another well but who carried out few, if any, joint activities. Kuman's social network was much larger and was more widespread and complex than
that of most Chimbu in Port Moresby. It was loose-knit in the
sense that the different sections within it had little or no
contact with one another,[1] but close-knit in that the separate
sections were very close-knit within themselves. Neither of
these two types of social network were similar to the social
networks Bott found among Londoners, but she did find that
segregation in the conjugal relationship went with segregation
in the couple's social network, which was the case with Kia
and Kuman.[2] The next section of this chapter shows that in

---

[1] Kuman's Papuan friends were mostly Motuans, Goilalas and
Keremas, who had very little contact with one another.

[2] See Chapter 8 for a discussion of how typical these types
of social networks and conjugal relationships were for families in category I or for all families in the sample.

comparison with Kuman and Kia, Kuman's brother and sister-in-law had a very different type of conjugal relationship, a difference due to individual personality differences rather than to social differences.

Individual choice. As described in Chapter 2, the experiences of one man in the Chimbu are very similar to those of every other man coming from the same part of the Chimbu. Kuman and Die had similar backgrounds and so had their wives. Neither man had any formal education, and both were polygynists, pagan and traditional in outlook. Both were very attached to their mother and were likely to have been similarly exposed to her influence. Both men had been to Port Moresby to work before, returning to Chimbu and coming back to Port Moresby. Both were working in similar jobs at the same institution.[1] But their personalities were very different.

When Die came to Port Moresby to work in 1967 he had already had four wives (three simultaneously for a time) and had divorced three of them. He brought with him a fifth wife, a young girl.[2] He said that he had married her because he was angry with Mol, his first and only remaining wife, because she had not borne him any chileren. After a few months Die sent the girl back to Chimbu 'because she did not cook properly or wash my clothes'. Soon after, Mol arrived in Port Moresby with Nol, an adopted daughter given to Die by his ex-(second) wife. 'Now', said Die, with intonations of affection in his voice, 'we two are just going to stay together even if we have no children. We are both getting old, and I'm not going to have any more wives'.[3]

---

[1] After my study was completed Die lost his job and had to undertake a different type of work.

[2] Mol, his first wife, was then in prison for fighting with Die's two previous wives in Chimbu because they had moved into a new house Die had built which she considered was for her alone. This, perhaps, indicates that Mol was a strong character, as well as being a physically strong woman, the latter probably because she had not had any children.

[3] It was said that when this couple were in Chimbu they behaved differently (i.e., each spouse frequently committed adultery and their activities were more segregated), a fact which if correct, supports Bott's (1971:92-6) suggestion that social environment affects the conjugal relationship.

Die, like Kuman, spent much time playing cards, but unlike Kuman, when Die went around town to find a card-playing group he nearly always took his wife with him.[1] He said that it would not be fair to go off and leave her, as 'Moresby is not her place'. When she had to work on Saturday mornings he usually stayed around the institution waiting for her to finish work so that they could go out together. Die seldom went out at night because he felt that it would attract trouble to walk around the city after dark with a woman. If they were already out visiting when it became dark they slept where they were visiting; otherwise they sat at home listening to the wireless.

Mol worked as a domestic servant and Die often did chores at home because she was working. However, two other social category I husbands whose wives were working never helped with domestic chores. Neither Die nor Mol gave much time to the little girl Nol but complained that she was disobedient. Mol belonged to a kampani[2] with two other Chimbu domestic servants. She spent her money as she pleased. She was always nicely dressed in a skirt and loose blouse. Earlier she used some of her earnings to pay the fare for her father to come and stay with her for a few months.

Kuman thought that when a wife is living with her husband, her husband is responsible for her; when she is living with her parents, they are in charge of her. This attitude came out very clearly when Kia came out of hospital and wanted to go back to Chimbu. Kuman would not agree, and when her uncle and cousin arrived from Chimbu they had to accept Kuman's decision. Die, on the contrary, seemed a little afraid of his parents-in-law. When both he and Mol wanted Mol to have an operation in the hope that she would have some children, her parents heard about it and objected. So she did not have the operation, much to the couple's disappointment. When I discussed the matter with Die he explained, 'We will be going back to Chimbu one day, and Mol's parents might kill me [through witchcraft] if she ever became sick. They would say that it was because of the operation'.

Die and Mol had fewer independently organised activities and more joint and complementary conjugal activities than did

---

[1] This could be the result of mutual interests, mutual distrust, or dominance of one partner over the other, and does not necessarily imply an emotional closeness between the spouses.

[2] Die belonged to a large kompani of Chimbu and said he would receive $200 when it was his turn to receive the member's contribution.

Kuman and Kia. By Bott's (1957:44, 45) definition we can say that they had a less segregated conjugal role-relationship than Kuman and Kia.

Die had the same large kin group as Kuman, and was a part of the large social grouping of Chimbu in Port Moresby. He wanted to move into a Housing Commission house so that his and Mol's kin could spend more time visiting them. He played cards and gambled and talked about matters of mutual interest but the actual content of his social relationships with the Chimbu was rather different to that of Kuman. This was indicated to me in a number of different ways and was due, I believe, to differences in the personalities of the two men.

When Chimbu came to the institution (about a mile out of town) where Kuman and Die and their families lived, with the exception of Mol's kinsmen they always went to Kuman's house and if they saw Die it would be because he had gone down to Kuman's house to see them. Die, I found, was a bit of a joke among his kinsmen, mainly because of his many amorous interests and adventures.[1] These, it seems, did not continue in Port Moresby because 'the girls here want too much money, even the old ones....And I might get sick'. But he maintained his interest and he liked to talk about the seamy side of life in Port Moresby, which sometimes annoyed Mol.

Die had one Papuan friend whom he met when he was in Port Moresby some years ago. This man came from the Koiari area inland from Port Moresby, and theirs was strictly a trading and economic relationship. Die went to this man's place to look for feathers for traditional gift-exchanges in Chimbu;[2] Die paid him for the feathers and gave him meals when he visited the city. Die sometimes played cards with Papuans in town, but he regarded such relationships as strictly business, for the purpose, he hoped, of making money. For Die there was not very much more to life than business and girls, although as he was getting older he seemed to be developing an

---

[1] As mentioned in Chapter 2, it is considered weakening and undesirable for Chimbu men to have much association or physical contact with women. This was not necessarily the only reason for people not regarding Die in a very serious light but it was certainly a very important factor.

[2] Many Chimbu in Port Moresby have similar relationships with Goilala and Kerema people.

emotional relationship with Mol.[1] Kuman was economically
orientated, as are all Chimbu, but he also had a feeling for
people, and his relationships with non-kin were more than
simply economic in content. Perhaps he got so much emotional
satisfaction from his dealings with the many people in his
social network that he did not need to depend upon his wife
(and children) for emotional satisfaction.

Die and Mol had a much more combined network than did Kia
and Kuman, and although Mol did not have much contact with
Die's Papuan friends she did see them sometimes. Mol spoke
Pidgin, but her social relationships were all with Chimbu,
her own relatives and some of the Chimbu working as domestic
servants to staff members of the institution where Die worked.
Most of these people know one another and also knew many of
the men in Die's social network, but they cannot be described
as an encapsulating social group, even though they did carry
out a few traditional activities together.

Apart from their visits to the hospital and their work
relationships with their employers, neither of these couples
had any relationships of the type Bott calls 'formal' relationships, i.e., with church groups, women's clubs, sports teams.
For the most part Die and Mol had a combined close-knit social
network of Chimbu, but Die had an additional loose-knit section of economic relationships with various Papuans, most of
whom Mol knew but with whom she had little direct interaction.
Because she usually went around with her husband, Mol had much
more direct contact with her affinal relatives than did Kia,
who kept in the background when Kuman's relatives came to
visit him.

A large part of Kuman's social network was the same as that
of Die and Mol and therefore had the same degree of connectedness (or density) although the relationships were different in
content. However, Kuman had a larger, more widespread network
than Die, a network which was hardly shared with Kia at all.
Theirs was a more segregated network, just as their conjugal
role-relationship was more segregated than that of Die and Mol.
Differences in the personalities of the two husbands, with
consequent differences in their personal decisions and choices,
largely account for the differences in their social networks

---

[1] In 1973 they had a big quarrel over one of Die's previous
wives who came down to Port Moresby and expressed a desire to
remarry Die. Mol returned to Chimbu but expected to come back
after one year. In the meantime, the previous wife was married
to someone else.

and in the degree of conjugal role segregation of the two
couples in a society where the socialisation of people is
relatively uniform and situational factors are similar. Related to this difference in the husbands were the personalities of their wives and how they reacted to their husbands'
personalities.

Chapter 6

Social category II families

Introduction

No specific features in the life-styles of all the category
II families differentiated them from the families in the other
two social categories. The differentiating characteristics
were specific to each family, but in all cases there was a
much sharper distinction between the families in categories II
and III than there was between the families in categories II
and I.

Domestic life

The families in social category II had a higher standard
of house, more material possessions and a higher income than
most but not all of the families in social category I. Their
houses had running water and electric power, wood or kerosene
stoves, and tubs for washing clothes. Two families regularly
ate off tables, while two usually sat on the floor to eat.
All slept on beds but none used sheets. However, in spite of
these material advantages, their domestic life was very similar
to that of the social category I families, except that not so
many kin were regularly involved.

Children

To a large degree the comments on children and child care
of the social category I families applied equally to social
category II families.[1] One couple no longer took their small
child to the pictures after she had become frightened and had
nightmares. The two elder children of one couple were being
brought up by the husband's sister. The younger one sometimes
visited his parents, but the older one had almost no direct
contact with them. However, the parents said the boys were
still theirs because they occasionally gave them pocket money

---

[1] See pp.55, 57-8.

Plate 11.   Low-covenant houses in an army compound.

and clothes.   This example illustrates the very direct relationship between economic and 'legal' ties in Chimbu social organisation, a relationship which pervades Chimbu thinking.[1]

Polygyny

One of the husbands who had two daughters said that if his
wife had another daughter it meant she had too much female
blood in her.   He would marry a second wife, becoming a polygynist, in order to have a son.[2]   He claimed it was in prepar-
ation for this eventuality that he had refused to marry in
church although he was previously a catechist and still had
close ties with the church.[3]

The other husbands and wives in this social category said
that they were not interested in polygyny, giving either
economic or religious reasons.

---

[1] See also p.81.

[2] Men want sons because traditionally they remain part of their
father's clan and live and work near to them due to land ties.
Daughters marry out of their natal group and go to live on
their husband's land.   It is sons, primarily, who look after
their fathers in old age.

[3] Husband K in social category I, whose wife was barren, made
a similar claim in explaining why he did not have a church
marriage.   He, too, had been a catechist.

Social networks

The families in this category were more individuated than those in category I, but less individuated than those in category III. They had smaller, less dense social networks of kin than did the families in category I, and were not so dependent upon their kin for a number of reasons. Three of the husbands had jobs where they were given leave fares by their employers, so they did not need to ask their relatives for money to purchase plane tickets to Chimbu if they wished to go home. Two husbands accepted, to varying degree , the army's ideology that a soldier's social relationships should be with other soldiers rather than with his own tribesmen, and that in times of need the army rather than his kinsmen would take care of him.[1] One of the husbands claimed that the Chimbu who visited his house all came to see his wife. Fear of witchcraft reprisals as a consequence of flouting kinship obligations was not an important consideration for these families while they lived in Port Moresby.

Army regulations determine who may live in the houses of its soldiers and for how long. In social category I some people who had kin working for the army were afraid to visit the army compound at any time although there was no restriction on such visiting during the day. Conversely a family in category III frequently obtained permission to stay with relatives in the army.

Those category II husbands who were not employed by the army had both evicted kinsmen from their houses at some time. In one case it was on the grounds that the kinsman, although working, was contributing nothing to the household - a common occurrence in social category I families but one which did not lead to the kinsman being evicted. Another husband said that he had evicted his kinsman and family because 'this man and his friends were always getting drunk and creating disturbances'. One of the wives evicted her relatives because she claimed, 'they had left her baby to cry when she and her husband had gone to the hospital'.

The husbands, and some of the wives, in category II had more social relationships with non-Chimbu than did the couples in category I. Husbands spent more time with workmates of any tribal origin. One family, which lived in a

---

[1] This is the ideology given by the men themselves. I am not in a position to say whether the army authorities would accept it as part of their ideology. I noted a number of exceptions in practice by the husbands making this claim.

low-cost housing settlement, had close ties with a number of
neighbours, none of whom were Chimbu. This particular family
had lived in Port Moresby for many years and in their present
house for over five years, and some of their neighbours had
been living near them for several years. Card-playing was one
of the main reasons for these social ties. In contrast, two
wives had almost no social contact with non-Chimbu women and
one gave up playing basketball because, she said, the Papuan
women dominated the teams and were not friendly towards the
Chimbu women who could not play so well.[1]

Some of the families had a few social relationships of the
type that Bott describes as formal social relationships.
These were business and professional relationships. Three
families had formal relationships with personnel of their
church. One family had some contact with their daughter's
teacher and another had regular contact with nursing sisters
at an infant welfare clinic, although the latter personnel
changed frequently.

To summarise, the main difference in the social networks
of the social category I and II families was that in the latter
there was less emphasis on kin relationships and more loosely
knit formal and informal social relationships with non-Chimbu.
This dimunition in the importance of kin in the social relationships of these families seemed to have little effect on conjugal relationships but did affect family organisation and permit the families more freedom of choice in spending their money.
The conjugal relationships of these families were as segregated
as most of those in social category I. One couple often watched football matches together and two couples frequently went
to church together. In contrast, one husband refused to go to
public gatherings with his wife because, he said, 'she talks
too much'. In three of the four families the spouses spent
very little time together.

Due to the general similarities in the life-style and social
relationships of category I and II families, a detailed case-
history of a social category II family is not included in this
presentation.

---

[1] The wife in one of the families which changed residence
during the research period quickly became friends with her
neighbours from Madang.

Chapter 7

Social category III families

Introduction

Only three families were included in category III. In only
two of the five sophisticated families I came in contact with
in Port Moresby were both husband and wife full-blooded Chimbu.
Of the three families I included, one of the husbands had left
his village to go away to school when he was eight years old
and the other two husbands both went to secondary boarding
schools either in Australia or in Papua New Guinea. All three
husbands had visited Australia. One wife had been brought up
on a mission station and educated in a boarding school; another
travelled to a number of different government stations with her
parents (her father was a government employee) and went to
different schools. The third wife left home to go to high
school and for tertiary training, but came home regularly for
holidays.

All these couples spoke English well. Two couples spoke
English at home because they wanted their children to learn
English. Two lived in high-cost housing with Western-type
furniture, and all regularly used chairs and tables. They
lived as nuclear families without relatives, but the wives did
not feel lonely or nervous during the day. One wife was working full-time, and the other two, in addition to housework and
child care, supplemented their husband's income by making
clothes for sale.

In spite of the relatively well paid positions that two of
the husbands had, they expected, hoped, eventually to return
to the highlands to live and work. To this end both were
interested in maintaining or obtaining rights in land. Land
is in short supply in the Chimbu. One husband had inherited
some, which he still owned, but he was worried that he might
lose it if he did not establish his rights by working the land.
The other husband had given his land to one of his brothers.
Consequently both he and his wife were overjoyed when the husband of a cousin who had plenty of land in another part of the

highlands offered them a sizable portion there with arrangements for individual title to the land. This land represented security and the opportunity to work for oneself rather than for an employer.

Marriage rites

All three families had free-choice marriages, although in one instance the initial suggestion came from the parents of both the girl and the boy and in another case expatriate teachers suggested to the young man that this particular girl might make a suitable wife for him. He followed up the suggestion by writing to the girl. The third couple had to overcome a certain amount of opposition from the girl's parents and kin before their marriage was agreed to.

Two husbands and all three wives were practising Christians; two couples had been married in church as well as according to traditional rites. In one case no brideprice was asked for the girl because the prospective husband was a student, and because the girl's father was satisfied with a very high brideprice that he had received for his other daughter.[1] This attitude was far removed from the traditional Chimbu attitude, and seemed to indicate an expectation expressed in other category III families (but not in the other social categories) that a young man today should be responsible for paying his own brideprice. Partly because this particular boy was unable to pay, the girl's father suggested that no brideprice be given. One of the other husbands paid brideprice for his wife himself, at the time of his marriage,[2] and the third paid his own, with the help of

---

[1] This father could make his own decision about the brideprice for his daughter because she had been brought up in boarding schools from an early age. In this part of the Chimbu, I was told by the wife concerned, relatives such as uncles usually make considerable contributions towards the feeding and decoration of young girls, in the expectation of being repaid when her brideprice is received. In this particular case the uncle was not very happy to let the girl go without brideprice, but he could not argue with the girl's father because he had not contributed to her upkeep nor given her presents, as she had been away at school. This was a new situation and way of thinking for the Chimbu.

[2] This would enhance his prestige among his own kinsmen and at the same time, although this may not have been a conscious motive, would mean that he was not placed under an obligation to those kinsmen who might otherwise have contributed towards his bride payment.

Plate 12. High-covenant accommodation with all modern conveniences, similar to that lived in by two category III families.

one uncle, some years after he had married 'to make my wife's relatives happy'.

In some African societies it has become customary for un-educated and little educated young men to give up their traditional roles and go to the towns to work for wages in order to pay their own brideprice (Phillips 1953, Yeld 1967). I noticed no such trend among the category I families in Port Moresby. Indeed, the kinsmen of one of the younger husbands in this group paid for his bride, and the fare for the girl and the boy's father to come to Port Moresby, without the bridegroom participating in any way. I am not sure that he knew that he was about to be married.

Polygyny

Polygyny is usually regarded as being incompatible with a companionate marriage (Clignet and Sween 1969) where the conjugal role-relationship is a joint one. However, some husbands and wives in category III, who showed evidence of a joint conjugal relationship, expressed ambivalent views on this form of marriage. None of the husbands had been polygynists, but the father of one husband had been a fight leader with many wives, and the uncle of one of the wives had been a polygynist. Both these men were admired by the husbands concerned.

One husband said that he saw nothing wrong in polygyny but
that he would not want to indulge in it because it would upset
his wife and he would not want to do that. 'And', he continued,
'Could I afford it? Probably not. And why should I have more
than one wife? No, I'm not really in favour of it, but I know
some educated, even high-school educated, men who have several
wives'.

Another husband said:

> It's not modern! [He wants to be modern.] Those
> educated men who have more than one wife are not
> really educated. It's not wrong; it depends upon
> circumstances, particularly economic circumstances.
> And a man must consider arrangements. If a man
> is rich he can do what he likes, but he has to con-
> sider family arrangements. He might still face
> problems. No, polygyny is not very good, and be-
> sides, my wife would kill me!!! [joking].

One of the wives began her discussion of polygyny by stat-
ing the church's opposition, and then discussed her own experiences in relation to polygyny:

> If a man wants to become a church member he must
> keep only one wife. This is very hard for the
> other wives, unless they have grown-up children to
> look after them. An uncle of mine had four wives,
> and they were all happy. He loved them all and
> was not willing to give up any of them although he
> wanted to join the church. No, there is nothing
> wrong in having more than one wife...[pause] but
> I wouldn't want my husband to take another wife;
> then he might not think of me and my children.
> But if I didn't have any children and he wanted
> another wife in order to have children, I would
> let him. [A pause.] Otherwise he might kill me
> [serious].

These views of people who have spent many years away from
traditional Chimbu society and influences, reflect the pragmatic Chimbu concept of the marriage relationship in terms of
practical economics, family arrangements and the production
of children, contrasting with the idealism of the Western
ideology of the companionate marriage. There was no suggestion that polygyny was morally wrong. The view that it was a
man's right to have children, coupled with the fear of being
killed either physically or by witchcraft, in the circumstances quoted, are strictly Chimbu concepts. But the Western
concept of love was also expressed several times: not wanting

to hurt one's wife, the uncle who loved all his wives so he
shouldn't have to give them up to join the church. Whether
love was also an element in the wife's conceding that if she
did not bear her husband any children she would have to allow
him to take another wife, I am unable to judge. Likewise it
is hard to interpret what exactly was intended when she said
'...then he might not think of me and my children' as a reason
for not wanting her own husband to be polygynist.

Views about polygyny among category I wives were less
ambivalent. Either they were in favour of polygyny and saw
practical advantages in the practice, or they were entirely
against it. 'How would you like it?' asked one, 'If your husband built a new house for the other wife, but not for you?'
But another said, 'I am old now. Let him take a young wife
to help me look after the children'. Most husbands who were
not already polygynists simply stated that the church forbade
them to have more than one wife, but that if it did not, then
when they went back to Chimbu they would marry more wives.

Clignet and Sween (1969), in their study of social change
and the incidence of polygyny in Abidjan, found that it was
not always among the most modern residents that the incidence
of polygyny was lowest. However, the emphasis and value placed
on polygyny seems to have been much greater in African than in
Papua New Guinean traditional societies.

Children

Category III parents took a great interest in their children. They played with them, read children's books with them,
looked for suitable pictures at the drive-in theatre to take
them to, and put on birthday parties for them, all these
activities being carried out on a family basis. These parents
had ambitions for their children, too: they wanted them to
learn English at an early age and go to primary 'A' schools[1]
rather than 'T' schools because they thought that this would
equip them better for the future.[2] For this reason they would

[1] Schools teaching the same syllabus as that taught in primary
schools in New South Wales instead of the Territory primary
school syllabus. Children who attend primary 'A' schools have
to speak English fluently.

[2] These schools were intended initially to be for overseas
children. However, in January 1973 the government stated that
from 1974 onwards it would not permit Papua New Guinean children to attend 'A' syllabus schools. It wants a single type
of education for all Papua New Guinean children (Post-Courier,
26 January 1973).

be unwilling to be posted to centres which did not have a
primary 'A' school.

Individuation

In comparison with the families in social category I, the
category III families were much more individuated, both physically and socially. Families in category I who lived in
households composed of one nuclear family, plus perhaps one
close relative, lived that way because of externally imposed
regulations and not from their own choice. The families in
category III lived as nuclear families from their own choice.
Each in their own way had dealt with the problem of obligations to kinsmen and people from their part of the Chimbu.[1]

Physical separation inhibited social dependence, particularly among people who did not have their own means of transport and who had little or no money to pay for public transport in such a scattered town as Port Moresby.[2] The large
homes of two of the category III families would probably have
inhibited some of their clansmen and prevented them from
visiting, particularly those who were not closely related and
therefore did not have a strong entitlement to assistance from
their more fortunate kinsmen. It would have been difficult
to find the houses in high-cost areas, areas with which unsophisticated clansmen might not be familiar. Such factors
diminished the demands made upon the category III families.

All three category III husbands declared that they did not
believe in witchcraft or sorcery, so that fear of retaliation
for not giving aid to kin would not have made it difficult to
refuse requests. Two of the wives believed that witchcraft
and sorcery were effective in the highlands, but did not think
that they existed among the Chimbu in Port Moresby.

One husband, who had political aspirations, said that it
would be bad to lose one's reputation by not assisting kin,
but his wife, who had few relatives in Port Moresby, was not
very sympathetic towards her husband giving assistance to his
relatives.

Two of the three families had their own car and the third
had regular access to one. This made it easy for them to do

[1] Social category II families were intermediate as far as
residence was concerned but two of the four families had to
obey institutional regulations.

[2] At the time of this study cheap public transport in Port
Moresby was very limited. Taxis were too expensive for the
social category I and II families except in emergencies.

things outside the home as a family, in contrast to the category I and II families who had transport difficulties.

Social networks

Most of the friends of the category III families had cars and visited them on a family-to-family basis. Many of these families knew and visited one another, so there was a close-knit network of combined husband-and-wife social relationships. The husbands and wives in category III first met most of their friends either at school or at work and most of them were of a similar education level. Many were related to one another, either affinally or consanguineously.

Families in category III selected kin in Port Moresby with whom they wished to maintain active social relationships. Most of those they interacted with had at least a primary school education, and several, both married and single, formed part of a single, close-knit social network together with the family's friends.

Formal social relationships were developed through the church or through the husband's work and included people of different tribes and races. Some involved both husband and wife, but many such relationships were with either the husband or wife.

John and Dubei

This family lived in a social environment very different from that of the families in social category I, but their conjugal role-relationship when analysed in terms of the concepts used by Bott seemed to be very similar to that of Die and Mol in social category I. This similarity raises a number of questions in relation to the concepts used and the method of analysis, and to the relative importance of social environment, education, income and personality factors in determining the type of conjugal role-relationship and/or the social network of a husband and wife.

John and Dubei had been married seven years. They had three children, two of their own and one adopted daughter. They lived in a rented, furnished, duplex home, one in a block of eight. All the other homes in the block were occupied by expatriates. John said that they came to live here because it was too noisy in the small flat in a low-cost housing suburb where they had lived previously. He denied that he moved to escape the demands of relatives, but said that the fact that the duplex was furnished, while a low-cost house could only be rented unfurnished, had been a factor. He said that

he did not want to buy his own furniture as he did not know
how much longer he would be living in Port Moresby.

John and Dubei did not have any friends among their neighbours, but they were friendly with parents of some of their
son's expatriate school friends at the primary 'A' school.
When I called at the house in the late afternoon or at weekends, John was often out in the garden playing ball with
Mitchell. One Saturday John and Dubei gave a birthday party
for their son, having sent out written invitations to Mitchell's
school-friends, and to the sons and daughters of their Papua
New Guinean friends. That afternoon the table was laden with
cakes, jellies, sandwiches and soft drinks, and beer was provided for those parents who stayed for the party. Children
in the category I and II families would never have experienced
anything like this unless possibly their parents were close
kin to a category III-type family and they were invited to go
along, but this would be unusual. This was not simply because
birthdays were not known among the unsophisticated families
but because child-focused activities were not part of Chimbu
culture.

The household. Originally, said John, he and Dubei decided,
for economic reasons, to have only one child, but then they
felt that it was not good that Mitchell had no one to share
with, so they decided to have one more child of their own.
Their adopted daughter was Dubei's youngest sister;[1] she was a
teenager who went out to work. She called Dubei 'Mum' and
John 'Dad', indicating that for Chimbu the social relationship has priority over the biological one, although of course
in most cases the two coincide. John and Dubei said they
adopted the girl because her father, who was not a Chimbu (he
lived on a mission station in the Chimbu for most of his adult
life and had married a Chimbu woman), had given the girl to
his own people so that they would not be angry with him and
harm him or his family (through witchcraft or sorcery). John
and Dubei said that the girl was not happy with her father's
people so they spoke to Dubei's father and he agreed to allow
them to adopt her.

John trained, and originally worked, as a clerk. In the
past Dubei had worked as a seamstress in a Chinese tradestore,
but during the time of my research she was at home looking
after her young daughter. She sewed a few clothes for private
sale. John, Dubei and the three children were the only people
living in the duplex.

---

[1] A similar adoption of a wife's younger sister had taken place
in a social category II family.

Financial arrangements. John told me that he did not want
any money that Dubei earned to be used for family or household
buying. 'I'm the father of the family and I must support my
family!' He said that he portioned out his earnings (about
$54 a fortnight) into food money, pocket money for Dubei and
Rachel (the adopted daughter), and money for rent and electricity. This arrangement was very similar to the arrangement
in the other category III family where the husband was the main
earner. In the third family the wife earned more than her husband and arrangements were a little different.

John and Dubei had separate bank accounts; Bott (1971:71,
79, 234) and some other social researchers use this as a criterion of segregation in a family's financial arrangements.
This idea is based on the argument that with separate accounts
each spouse controls his or her money independently of the
other spouse. I believe that to some extent this manifestation
of independence in the spouses' financial arrangements may be
modified by the way that the spouses each spend their money.
Each may spend it for joint needs, joint activities, joint
pleasures. They may regard it as family finance even if each
has his or her money in separate accounts.

When Kia earned money she spent it on herself or on things
for her kin, but Kuman did not give her a personal allowance
even when she was not earning money. There was no co-operation
in the handling of their finances. John gave Dubei a personal
allowance as well as money for food, and, said Dubei, he never
asked her for money. She did, however, help him sometimes without being asked, by paying the rent or the electricity bill,
i.e., she helped or co-operated with her husband on her own
initiative.

Rachel, who earned $28 a fortnight, sometimes bought food
or gave money to Dubei for the purchase of food. At other
times she asked for money if she needed some. John said that
he was always very cautious about giving money to kinsmen who
asked him for help, inquiring as to whether they have been
working, and if not why not, and then deciding whether they
merited his assistance.

None of the spouses in the category III families belonged
to a kampani. One of the husbands had gambled considerably
in the past, but his wife claimed that he had now given it up.
Two of the husbands were moderate drinkers, the third seldom
drinking. One of the wives was very fond of wine. Kuman and
Die in category I were only moderate drinkers, but some of the
other husbands in that social category drank very heavily, in
spite of their low wages.

Marriage history. John explained that he had always expected that he himself would pay brideprice for his wife when he married. Hence when he was working he always sent money home to his relatives, knowing that, in accordance with Chimbu custom, they would give him back the exact equivalent when he needed it to pay for his bride. None of the other husbands told me of doing this, but some of the husbands in category I had probably given services to their kinsmen which could be regarded in the same light as the money that John sent to his kin.

John claimed that he and Dubei knew each other well before their marriage but this was through correspondence only. They first met face to face at the time of their marriage. Dubei's parents were against the marriage at first because, they said, John was really Dubei's uncle. Dubei says that she talked them into agreeing to the marriage by declaring that she was not a true Chimbu as her father was not a Chimbu and she and her brothers and sisters had become members of her mother's lineage in special circumstances, that is, she argued in terms of biological not social relationships.[1] She and John were married both in church and by traditional rites.

Conjugal relationship. As mentioned, John and Dubei did many things together as a family. I asked John what he thought were the characteristics of a good wife, and he immediately suggested the following: she must spend money for the good of the whole family and not just for herself; she must entertain her husband's visitors, even if they come at an inconvenient time; she must be a good cook; she should take part in community affairs. He was a little taken back at being asked what he thought were the characteristics of a good husband. After a little thought, he suggested the following, saying

> I don't know whether I do all these, but this is
> what I think: He must look after his wife and chil-
> dren and provide them with food and clothes [John
> said a wife needed good clothes in Port Moresby]

---

[1] Children normally belong to their patrilineage except when their parents are divorced and the husband is blamed for the failure of the marriage. Every child must belong to a lineage, but as the members of Dubei's father's lineage lived far away and took no part in the family's social life, it was decided that Dubei and her siblings should become members of their mother's patrilineage. It was only as a result of this unusual circumstance that John would be considered to be an uncle of Dubei.

and save money for the family; he must make his
wife and children happy, and go to parties or spend
money on drink only after he has provided them with
all the things they need; when he goes out he
should let his wife know where he is going, and he
should take the family out to watch football matches
and to parties.

Most of these suggestions were very different from those
suggested by husbands in categories I and II: for these husbands a good wife should be obedient and work hard; no con-
sistent suggestions were made about a good husband, and many
husbands found the question difficult to answer.

A number of times during our discussions John mentioned the
importance of husband and wife talking things over together,
rather than getting angry about things and each always wanting
to do something different. He stressed the importance of looking after the children and also mentioned that a wife should
be economical.[1]

In these concepts of John's there are some features that
are characteristically Chimbu and others which seem more
characteristic of middle-class Western society's family relationships.[2] The stress laid on entertaining one's husband's
relatives or visitors and on being economical are, I feel,
Chimbu traits. Consultation between husband and wife, the
importance of considering the happiness and welfare of the
nuclear family, the suggestion that a wife should take part
in community affairs, seem more characteristic of the Western
companionate-type marriage than of Chimbu marriage, with its
strict division of labour between husband and wife, and stress
on patrilineage interests. Similar responses came from the
other category III families. One wife discussed the difficulties of wives in town finding ways to help their husbands.
She came to the conclusion that the only way for her to help
her husband was to be friendly to his visitors. One husband
who seemed to have been influenced by glossy magazines, said
'A good wife? She must be good-looking... very important!
And she must be intelligent!' 'A good husband? You tell me!

---

[1] He told me on one occasion that he was very proud of Dubei
because she was so economical.

[2] This is not to imply that any of these characteristics are
necessarily exclusive to either Chimbu or Western family
relationships.

Well... for a European he must have a good job. For a Chimbu
he must have lots of things!''[1]

   All the category III husbands helped their wives with
domestic chores, although Dubei complained that while John was
prepared to cook or help look after the children, he would not
clean the house. In Chimbu men cook certain types of food
(pig, pandanus) and spend time with children. I doubt that
house cleaning has a traditional equivalent. Leaves on the
floor of the houses are replenished from time to time, and
after a few years people move to a new house and the old house
either falls down or is burnt down.

   None of these couples wanted a large family. One wife was
taking 'the pill', one couple said they were practising self-
control and abstaining from sexual intercourse, while the
third husband said that his wife could go to the family planning clinic if she wanted to, but he had no time to go.[2]

   Social networks. John had a considerable number of social
relationships of the type Bott calls formal external relationships. These were connected with his work, his political
interests, his church, and to a lesser extent the hospital
(after Mitchell had had an accident) and the teachers at
Mitchell's school. Dubei also had some external formal relationships, some with the same people as John but a few with
people whom John did not know (members of the church women's
association or women for whom she did dressmaking). For the
most part theirs was a combined, closely knit network of
friends, with additional combined and segregated formal relationships. The friends were past school-mates, past or
present work-mates of John's (many related directly or through
marriage to either John or Dubei), or from the kin group of
either John or Dubei. John and Dubei selected which members
of their kin group in Port Moresby they wished to maintain
social relationships with, something which the couples in
category I did not usually do.

---

[1] This husband did not specify whether he was referring to
traditional, rural Chimbu, or to men such as himself. Probably the main difference between the two would be the type of
things a man would need to have. In any event the basic
principle expressed is the same for Chimbu or Westerner, because although the latter needs a good job primarily for purchasing 'things' it may also bring status, etc. However, the
difference in emphasis is interesting.

[2] It is the policy of the family planning programme in Papua
New Guinea to interview both husband and wife.

In a number of respects the social network of John and Dubei was similar to that of Die and Mol. It was a combined, closely knit network with a core group of kin relationships within it, but with some external relationships with non-Chimbu. The main differences seemed to be that John and Dubei selected which kin they would maintain relationships with rather than all kin automatically being part of the social network, as was the case with Die and Mol. In addition, John and Dubei had many more formal social relationships than Die and Mol. Finally, Mol had no social relationships with non-Chimbu while Dubei had a considerable number.

Many of the people with whom John and Dubei had formal relationships knew each other well, so this part of the network was fairly closely knit, and many of these people also knew John and Dubei's friends. This is a type of conjugal relationship and social network pattern not seen by Bott in her study: a joint conjugal relationship and a closely knit social network. Die and Mol seemed to exhibit the same pattern, with possibly a less joint conjugal relationship and less closely knit social network. However, the motivations seemed to be different in the two couples, John and Dubei being more family oriented while Die and Mol were individually and lineage-oriented.

Chapter 8

Social networks of urban families

Introduction

In the Chimbu single men and girls and influential married men often visit kinsmen, trade-partners and people in friendly clans. Married women regularly stay with their natal kin, but husbands and wives seldom visit together except as part of a larger kin group participating in a special function, such as a funeral. This pattern was maintained in Port Moresby, particularly among the families in social categories I and II, except that wives could not visit natal kin very often if, as was frequently the case, her close kin were living in Chimbu.

A succession of single men, or married men whose wives were in Chimbu, dropped in to see most of the category I and II families studied, especially at weekends. Sometimes they stayed only for ten minutes, long enough to let their kin know that they were well and to see that their kin were well in themselves, or to greet a new arrival from Chimbu; at other times they stayed all day, all night, and most of the following day, and some stayed indefinitely. Frequently a group of three to five men or more arrived together; the hosts might not know all their names or what, if any, blood or affinal relationship they had to them. They only knew that they were Chimbu, and that they came to visit them with someone whom they did know.

Sometimes a group of ten or more men arrived to play cards. Often none of these men were known to the householder and his wife, although they knew that they were Chimbu. Little or no social intercourse took place, for the visitors did not come to visit anyone: they just moved around from house to house playing cards. They did this to avoid police detection. Sometimes one of the card players was acquainted with the householder; sometimes the householder himself might join in the card playing. Assessing this type of social relationship and its content is difficult in situations such as these. Can it, in fact, be described as a social relationship?

93

The use of kinship and other terms relative to a particular situation rather than as an absolute term makes the analysis of the kinship content of social networks difficult. Particularly for quantitative purposes, to make an accurate analysis would require much probing, which might antagonise or bore the informants - the Chimbu not being very interested in the details of kinship relationships - and would certainly be extremely time-consuming and tedious. It is not simply the difficulty in determining whether the use of a particular term in a particular instance denotes a known blood or affinal link between two people or whether the term is used only in the urban situation because both speak the same language. Kinship terms, and other terms of address, indicate the nature of a social relationship between two people rather than a special consanguinial or affinal tie. However, in the same way that the term itself is used relatively, so is the behavioural content denoted by the term. For example, the term 'brother' does not mean that the behaviour between people calling each other brother is the same although there will be some characteristics common to all 'brother relationships'. Variations tend to be in degree rather than kind.

In certain situations in Port Moresby all Chimbu regarded all other Chimbu as brothers, but the degree of 'brotherly involvement' would be less for those who were not fellow clansmen than it would be for those who were. In a different context non-clansmen might not be considered brothers, but clansmen would be. On the grounds that in some contexts all Chimbu in Port Moresby regarded all other Chimbu as brothers, instead of trying to distinguish between different kin relationships within a family's social network, I have classified the relationships in these networks into one of three kinds: social relationships with Chimbu, formal social relationships, and social relationships with non-Chimbu.

The social relationships of the category III families were different to those of families in the other two categories in a number of respects. The category III families frequently visited as a family group and family groups came to visit them. This was facilitated by their ownership of, or access to, a car; many of their friends also had cars. Category I and II spouses interacted as individuals rather than as families.

Bott (1971:103-5) discusses the importance of neighbours in the social networks of London families with segregated conjugal role-relationships. These families had lived in the same neighbourhood all their lives and husbands and wives came from families who also lived, or had lived, in the same neighbourhood.

All the Chimbu families in Port Moresby had left their
neighbourhood of birth, and many of the social category I and
II families changed their place of residence once, or more
during my study.[1] This meant that their neighbours changed.
Only four families, A, H, O and P, developed social relationships with non-Chimbu neighbours. In A's case these relationships were minimal but practical.[2] Of the four families which
did not move house only one had social relationships with non-
kin neighbours. In the shanty settlements people had little
contact with people from different parts of the Chimbu and
restricted their relationships to their closest neighbours,
who would be people from the same area, people who were usually
related to them by blood or affinal links.

Social relationships with
other Chimbu

Most of the families' social relationships were with Chimbu,
the proportion of relationships with non-Chimbu being highest
in the social category III families. In categories I and II
only two wives had any non-Chimbu relationships.

In only three of the twenty families (none in category I)
did both husband and wife claim to have no close relatives in
Port Moresby. Most people had clansmen in the city; those
with no relatives identified themselves with people who came
from the same place in Chimbu.

Bott (1957:289) distinguishes a social network from an
organised group mainly on the basis that there is a lack of
a common boundary in a social network, that is, a lack of
'agreement by all members of the group on who is and who is
not a member'. She also mentions (1971:58) that an organised
group makes up 'a... social whole, with common aims, inter-
dependent roles....' On the basis of these definitions, it
would not be accurate to describe the social relationships of
even the category I families in Port Moresby as forming a group.
Kinship relationships were extended to other Chimbu on an

---

[1] See pp.49-50. Families A and M were in category I, and O and
P in category II.

[2] For example, when one house had its water cut off, a hose
brought water from the neighbour's house. When the other
house had its electricity cut off, an extension lead took
light to it from the other house. When a fight took place
in A's house, neighbours took in his children for the night.
But A's children did not know to which tribal group these
neighbours belonged.

individual or close kin group basis, rather than by all the people with whom an individual had social relationships. Consequently there were no common boundaries in the social relationships of the families studied. Relationships with non-Chimbu were almost always on an individual rather than group basis. However, if it is accepted that there is a continuum ranging from social groups to close-knit social networks, then Chimbu families in the Chimbu could be classified as being part of a social group; while the families in social category I in Port Moresby would lie on the social-group border of the close-knit social network classification, and social category II and III families would fall further along the scale towards loose-knit social networks.

The social category III families selected the relatives with whom they maintained relationships and their networks of Chimbu were small compared with those of many category I families. They spent little time with uneducated Chimbu, but might meet them at church or at political gatherings. Even within the educated group of Chimbu they maintained close relationships only with people they personally liked. Category II families also selected relationships, but two families' social relationships were modified by their employers' rules.

The social category III couples had joint relationships with both Chimbu and non-Chimbu. In the other categories husbands and wives had more separate social relationships, or one part of the husbands' networks was combined with that of their wives, and the other part was separate. In social category III husbands and wives had more combined networks.

Formal social relationships

Table 8.1 shows the organisations with which the families had formal relationships. No indication of the intensity of the relationships is provided. Church and church fellowship meetings were the most frequent kind of formal social relationships. Church was a weekly event, and apart from the case of wife R, fellowship meetings were also attended weekly.

In her analysis of formal relationships Bott mentions (1971:65) that the wife of the couple with a close-knit social network was reticent about visiting doctors and hospitals. As Bott had only one such family in her sample this may have been an idiosyncratic manifestation. The families I studied nearly all had close-knit social networks, although sometimes the husband and the wife each had their own separate close-knit network. However, they did not seem nervous about going to the hospital or taking their infants to the baby clinics.

Table 8.1

Formal relationships

Family	Church	Church fellow-ship*	Baby clinic	Hospital	Sport	Pic-tures	Court
Social category I:							
A	-	-	-	A	-	-	-
B	B**	-	-	-	-	-	B***
C	-	-	-	-	-	-	-
D	-	-	-	D≠	-	-	-
E	-	-	-	-	-	-	-
F	F	F	-	-	-	-	-
G	G	G	-	-	-	-	-
H	H	H	H**	-	-	-	H***
I	I	I	-	-	-	-	-
J	-	-	-	-	-	-	-
K	-	-	-	-	-	-	-
L	-	-	-	-	-	-	-
M	M	M	M**	-	-	-	-
Social category II:							
N	N**	-	-	-	N	-	-
O	-	-	O**	-	-	-	-
P	P	-	-	-	-	-	-
Q	-	-	-	-	-	Q**	-
Social category III:							
R	R	R**	-	R	R***	-	-
S	S	S	-	-	S***	-	-
T	T**	-	-	-	-	T	-

* Fellowship meetings were held once a week by husband G at his home, and everyone at the compound household (including families G, H and I) was obliged to attend. Husband M also had fellowship at his house.

** Wife only.

*** Husband only.

≠ I doubt whether this couple would have gone to the hospital if I had not taken them in my car.

When they did not go, it was more likely to be because of
lack of interest, or lack of transport, or the long wait at
the clinic, rather than because they felt nervous.

Five of the thirteen families in social category I had
no formal relationships, all families in category II had at
least one formal relationship, and all social category III
families had more than one. Had there been any reason for
families S or T in category III to need the services of a
doctor or hospital they would not have hesitated to go;
this would not necessarily have been the case with the category I families.[1] However, if any of these wives had been
about to give birth to a child it is probable their husbands
or relatives would have seen that they went to hospital.

With regard to court involvement, one man was arrested
during the time of my study for being drunk and disorderly;
another went to court to pay a fine imposed on one of his
relatives.

Table 8.1 does not indicate with which people the families were involved in formal situations. Most of the people
they met in church and had social intercourse with were
people they already knew in other contexts. This might also
apply to the church fellowship relationships. Social relationships made at sports meetings, in the clinic or hospital or at court were likely to be formal in Bott's sense
of the term, and to represent a loose-knit section of the
families' social networks. I am not sure that any formal
social relationships are formed when people go to the pictures.

Social relationships with
non-Chimbu

Chimbu are sometimes regarded as being aggressive, quarrel-
some people. Certainly many Papuans in Port Moresby said
they were afraid of Chimbu and thought they caused much of
the social tension and violence in the city. It was therefore a little surprising to find that many of the husbands
had social relationships with people of other tribes living
in Port Moresby. Some of these relationships were formed

---

[1] As mentioned, the child in family E was not taken to hospital, although the mother and the father's kinsmen wanted
her to go, because the child did not want to go. In another
instance, a child was not taken to hospital because the father
was at work and the mother had no transport and no money for
the fare.

years earlier, when there were fewer Chimbu in the city; perhaps at that time they did not have their present reputation
for violence. Also, this was before the change in the law
which made it legal for Papua New Guineans to drink alcoholic
beverages. Some of the men were only boys when they first
came to Port Moresby. If they were married they did not have
their wives, families or close relatives with them. I suspect that some of the Papuans in the city felt that they would
be lonely, and therefore extended friendship to them.

Most relationships with non-Chimbu were specific to each
individual husband or wife and were not part of their tightly
knit network of relationships with Chimbu. They were similar
in many respects to the trading-partner relationship of the
Chimbu.

Three wives, H, O and P formed independent relationships with
non-Chimbu women because they felt the need for female company. Most of the husbands' relationships with non-Chimbu
had some economic content, but friendship was also important.
For example, husband C had a Kerema drinking partner whom he
originally met at work. As they now both worked for different
companies and were paid on alternate Fridays, husband C paid
for the drinks one weekend, and the following weekend his
Kerema friend paid!

Table 8.2 sets out non-quantitative information about the
Chimbu couples' relationships with non-Chimbu.

A comparison of the social networks of families in different social categories

The social networks of the urban Chimbu families in categories I and II were basically similar to those of rural
Chimbu. In Port Moresby people from the same place or language
group often filled in gaps in the network which resulted from
part of man's kin group or clan being in Chimbu. Thus, social
networks in these categories were close-knit and fairly widespread. These relationships were less political and social
and probably more economic and emotional in content than those
of the rural people: in the urban environment the political
and social activities of the Chimbu as a group were diminished,
and economic considerations and the need for emotional support
in a strange, competitive and sometimes hostile social and
physical environment were accentuated. Formal social relationships were very few and non-Chimbu relationships were restricted to one or two people.

The social networks of the category II families emphasised
kin relationships less than did those of category I families.

Table 8.2

Non-Chimbu relationships*

Family	Type of relationship	Tribe	Remarks
Social category I:			
A**	(i) Card players	Motu, Kerema	Friendly and economic. Known for many years.
	(ii) Neighbours	Unknown	Friendly, mutual aid.
B	-	-	-
C**	Drinking partner	Kerema	Met him at work
D	-	-	-
E	-	-	-
F**	Adopted as a kinsman	Koiari	They adopted him as a young man.
G	-	-	-
H***	Friend	Hula	Neighbour
I	-	-	-
J**	Friend-trade	Koiari	Husband hunted birds with him.
K**	Customers in business	Motu, Hula	-
L**	Card players	Motu, Kerema	Business relationships
M	-	-	-
Social category II:			
N**	Army mates	Territory-wide	Drinking, work, etc.
O**	Husband O was a Kerema man	Kerema	He now considered himself a Chimbu, but visited his sister
O***	Wife O friends with neighbours	Buka married to Madang	
P≠	Card players, friends	Kerema, Finschhafen	Neighbours
Q**	Army mates	Territory-wide	Drinking, work
Social category III:			
R≠	Friends	Various educated, e.g., Sepik, mixed-race, highlanders	Met at school and work
S≠	Congregation members	Finschhafen#	Came to the Chimbu with missionaries
T≠	Friends	Various educated, e.g., Sepik, Manus, European	Met at school or work

* See Appendix C for more information about many of the Kerema relationships.

** Husband only.

*** Wife only.

≠ Husband and wife.

There were also many Lae people in the congregation, but, it was stated, Lae people and Chimbu do not get on well.

Restrictions upon relatives living in institutional houses were welcomed by category II families but not by those in category I.

Families in social category III had fewer kin networks than those in category II. In many respects they were more like the networks of the London families than those of other Chimbu families. The couples were even more selective than category II families in their choice of kin with whom to have close ties; casual kin relationships were avoided as much as possible.

The category III families had a small close-knit network of friends and some kin with whom they exchanged visits on a family-to-family basis. In times of trouble the families went for assistance to kin within this network. In addition to this small combined network of friends and kin, there was a fairly loose-knit network of formal relationships, most of these being relationships of the husbands, originating at work or in community organisations. Common political interests formed the nucleus of another section of some families' social networks; many of the people involved might also be friends of kin. Wives had small sections of church-based relationships within their social networks.

Quantitative analysis of social networks

Bott (1971:61) suggests that a great deal of information, both qualitative and quantitative, must be collected about the social relationships of families and family members (Bott does not always make it clear to which she is referring,[1] before a satisfactory analysis of family social networks can be made. Gluckman (Bott 1971:xxvi) in his preface to the second edition of Bott's book states:

> We need...to specify carefully the content of re-
> lationships within the network, and the purposes
> they serve. Mere friendship is not enough as a
> means of linking persons in a network.

Bott (1957:61) states that she and Robb did not collect adequate information for a quantitative analysis of the social networks of the London families which they studied. The same is true of my study of Chimbu families living in Port Moresby.

---

[1] Barnes (1972:22,23) takes the view that Bott refers to a couple's network as comprising relationships with other couples, or an individual spouse's relationships with other individuals. I have not taken this view, and consider that networks may be comprised of relationships with both couples and individuals.

There are many difficulties involved in the collection and interpretation of data on social relationships for the purpose of network analysis. Some of these difficulties apply cross-culturally, such as the problem of determining and measuring all the various motivations involved in social interaction between people, a difficulty which is aggravated if the analyst is of a different culture to that of the people being studied. Other difficulties are specific to a particular situation; for example, when a person visits a compound household it may be difficult to assess whom he has come to visit and for what purposes. In the case of the Chimbu families being studied, a very large problem was that the families did not always know the names or the biological relationship - if any - of some of their visitors. They simply knew that they were Chimbu.

The data which I collected was adequate to permit a differentiation of the characteristics of the social networks of category I and III families. It was not, however, adequate for a quantitative analysis, which would need to include an analysis of the intensity, frequency and content of the various social relationships making up the social networks of the families studied.

Chapter 9

Quantitative analysis of conjugal relationships-
activities and behaviour

Introduction

Bott (1971:61) suggests that, in order to test her hypothesis that there is a direct relationship between the degree
of segregation in the conjugal role-relationship and the density of the husband and wife's social network, the information
about these social relationships must be quantified and the
families placed on a scale according to their degree of conjugal role segregation. She herself did not quantify her data
because, she claimed, she and her co-interviewer did not make
exactly the same observations nor ask the same questions of
each couple, although they did try to keep their interviews
as uniform as possible.

The basic information collected from the twenty urban Chimbu
families was the same in each case, and in accordance with the
outline presented in the interview guide.[1] Only the supple-
mentary data varied from family to family, the spontaneous information being provided by husbands and/or wives during conversations. The information collected was classified under a
number of headings and attempts were made to analyse activities
relevant to each heading in terms of joint, complementary or
independent organisation. Unfortunately it was not always
possible to do this satisfactorily for all the families, due
to the nature of the activities being quantified and the in-
herent methodological difficulty of distinguishing between
norms of behaviour and actual behaviour when information is
collected by asking people what they do rather than by observing directly what they are doing.

Activities

Activities of the husband and wife were classified as
follows:

---

[1] See Appendix A.

(i)   Financial arrangements
    (ii)   Domestic work
   (iii)   Child care
    (iv)   Leisure activities
    (v)   The sexual relationship

The small number of activities that many husbands and wives performed meant that the number which could be used for tabulating purposes and for the purpose of assessing conjugal-role relationships in terms of their degree of segregation was minimal. This fact in itself is an expression of a lack of jointness in the conjugal relationship, that is, there are few things for spouses to do together.

Financial arrangements

In this context jointly organised activities were those where the husband and wife discussed their financial arrangements and agreed how money earned by either was to be spent. Complementary activities were those where the husband and wife decided together that one or other would control all or most of the money earned by either. In such cases the degree of control by either spouse was not assessed, for example, whether or not money was automatically given to the other spouse when asked for, regardless of how it was to be spent. Independent financial organisation was where there was no consultation between husband and wife about how the money either earned was spent. The earner spent it as he or she wished, but might give some to the other spouse either to spend as he or she wished or to be spent for particular purposes.

Bott used the question 'Does the wife know how much the husband is earning?' as one criterion for assessing the type of financial arrangement existing between a husband and his wife. Some Chimbu wives in Port Moresby believed that they knew how much their husband was earning but their information was incorrect.[1] Overtime variations or frequent changing of jobs made it more difficult for some wives than others to know with any degree of accuracy what their husband's income was. Answers to this question as a means of assessing the degree of jointness or segregation in a couple's financial organisation might be misleading in the case of Chimbu couples and for this reason it was not used in my assessment.

---

[1] This could also have been true of the London wives, but Bott (1971) does not raise this possibility.

The results in Table 9.1 do not indicate any strong relationship between social category and the arrangement of family
finances, although the only joint arrangements were in categories II and III. Joint arrangement of family finances appears
to be unusual among the Chimbu in Port Moresby.[1] Independent
organisation by the earner was more common, particularly of
the wife's income when she worked. For those wives who had
no income of their own, such an arrangement would contribute
to their feeling of insecurity, dependence and economic in-
sufficiency in the urban environment, in contrast to their
situation in Chimbu.

There was no relationship between size of income and arrangements for spending it. The families with the highest incomes
were K (independent), T (joint), F (complementary) and R (independent). The lowest incomes were in families D (complementary) and I (independent); husband D sometimes spent most
of his pay on the way home, so his family saw very little of
it.

When Chimbu wives came to Port Moresby they either did not
participate in economic production for the family, or if they
did, they seldom did so in co-operation with their husbands
and this was a major factor in changing the husband/wife relationship in town. It was a divisive factor in that the husband was no longer dependent in any way upon his wife for her
contribution in economic production, while she was completely
dependent upon him. In Port Moresby a wife in social category
I and II families was likely to be an economic liability,
while in Chimbu she was an economic asset to her husband. Most
husbands felt that they could, and many did so for several
years, manage without the domestic or sexual services of a wife
in Port Moresby.[2] The social relationships consequent upon a
marriage are maintained regardless of whether the wife is in
Chimbu or Port Moresby, although exchanges may be modified.

In contrast, the husband's role in economic production made
the wives economically dependent upon their husbands, a relationship which the wives found unpleasant, and which the
husbands did not always accept in a responsible manner. The
wife was in a vulnerable position, particularly if she did not
have a brother, or a classificatory brother, in Port Moresby

---

[1] See p.   for the traditional basis for this practice.

[2] As mentioned in Chapter 2, traditionally wives were not regarded as companions or as sources of emotional satisfaction.

Table 9.1

Financial arrangements and mode of control

Family	Husband's income		Wife's income		Final assessment
	Mode of control	Kampani member	Mode of control	Kampani member	
Social category I:					
A	Independent	Yes	Independent	No	Independent
B	Complementary	No*	Independent	No	Complementary
C	Independent	Yes	n.a.**	n.a.	Independent
D	Complementary	No	n.a.	n.a.	Complementary
E	Independent	Yes	n.a.	n.a.	Independent
F	Complementary	No	Complementary***	No	Complementary
G	Independent	No	n.a.	n.a.	Independent
H	Independent	No	n.a.	n.a.	Independent
I	Independent	Yes	n.a.	n.a.	Independent
J	Complementary	Yes	Independent	Yes	Complementary
K	n.a.	n.a.	Independent ≠	No	Independent
L	Independent	No	n.a.	n.a.	Independent
M	Complementary	No	n.a.	n.a.	Complementary
Social category II:					
N	Joint/complementary≠	No	n.a.	n.a.	Joint
O	Independent	No	n.a.	n.a.	Independent
P	Independent	No	n.a.	n.a.	Independent
Q	Independent	No	n.a.	n.a.	Independent
Social category III:					
R	Independent	No	Independent	No	Independent
S	Complementary	No	Complementary##	No	Complementary
T	Joint	No	n.a.	n.a.	Joint

* Husband B regularly exchanged a small proportion of his salary with another man.

** Not applicable.

*** Both the husband and wife were working. In addition, they had two businesses,
a passenger truck and a small pig farm. They had separate bank accounts for each
spouse had his/her own account. The husband had overall control of all these
accounts, but there was a good deal of informal discussion about the expenditure
of money from any of the accounts.

≠ The wife's earnings were controlled by her husband without her consent and to
some extent against her wishes.

\# Some of the husband's income was handed over to his wife to control, but in
practice he could spend it as he wished.

\#\# The wife earned more than her husband, which might explain why there was joint
consultation about how both their incomes would be spent.

to look after her interests.[1] The division of labour within
the family was thus upset, and this may be the reason many
husbands and wives preferred the wife to remain in Chimbu
while the husband worked in Port Moresby. This suggestion,
however, needs further investigation.

A kampani[2] member puts most earnings into the kampani for
a number of weeks, the husband usually giving his wife a few
dollars for the family's food each fortnight. When the husband receives payments from the other kampani member there
are several possible arrangements for spending the money: the
husband may spend the money as he wishes; he and his wife may
decide jointly how they will spend it (if it is a large amount
some almost certainly will be given to kinsfolk in Port Moresby
or in Chimbu to repay debts or to maintain ties); or it is
possible, but unlikely, that the husband will hand most of it
over to his wife for her to spend as she thinks fit.

Although I have information on the way couples spent such
money, I do not know the basis on which, or the reason why,
the husband joined the kampani in the first instance. The
only wife who belonged to a kampani joined with her husband's
approval, but I consider it unlikely that the husbands discussed with their wives whether they should join a kampani.
Except for family J where the wife was also working and belonged
to a kampani, the husbands who belong to kampani were ones where
there was independent organisation of the family income. None
of the spouses in social categories II and III belonged to a
kampani.

Domestic work

Of the seven activities that could be used as criteria to
measure the degree of role segregation in the domestic sphere,
four were applicable to all families: cooking, washing-up,
washing clothes and cleaning the house. Work in the garden
applied to all but four families, chopping and collecting firewood to all but three, and the carrying of water applied to
only six families (all in category I), the remainder having
piped water either in or close to the house, or so far away

---

[1] See p. . Most category I wives were too traditionally
oriented, or too ignorant of the city's government or church
facilities to seek support from them, just as these organisations themselves may not be geared to provide support in
a manner that would be considered appropriate by the women
themselves.

[2] For details of kampani, see p. .

that they rarely brought any quantity to their house. I
omitted the water-carrying activity as it applied to so few
families.

Cooking, cleaning the house, and collecting and chopping
firewood, are all undertaken in the Chimbu, and there are institutionalised norms regarding their performance. Gardening
in Port Moresby has a different significance to gardening in
Chimbu; washing clothes is an introduced activity.

Six domestic tasks are very few on which to base an assessment. In the shanty settlements and low-cost houses most
people lived and slept in the same clothes, and had no bedding
other than a mat and perhaps a light blanket. Rolling up a
blanket or sleeping mat hardly merits the description of a
domestic task, and sometimes it was not rolled up all day.

Table 9.2 shows that more joint and complementary domestic
and gardening activities were carried out by the families in
social categories II and III than in social category I families.[1] Category I families in which domestic tasks were jointly performed were those where the wife worked for money. This
did not mean, however, that in all families where the wife
worked for money the husband participated in household tasks.

Three husbands helped their wives by bringing firewood home
or chopping large pieces of timber. Two of these husbands
were from Sinasina, and the other from an area near Sinasina.
Traditionally the division of labour between the sexes and
other aspects of male-female tension were apparently less
marked in Sinasina than in other parts of the Chimbu.[2]

In classifying domestic activities, I included as joint
activities only those regularly performed by both spouses
rather than those which a spouse performed only sporadically,
when there was a particular need, for example, when the other
spouse was very busy. This is in keeping with Bott's concepts,
although she does not discuss this nor the problem of how to
distinguish help given by one spouse to the other from a joint
activity.

---

[1] No husband in the sample washed clothes, and only one, who
had lived in Australia for two years, regularly cleaned the
house. See also p. .

[2] As mentioned in Chapter 2, east of the Chimbu River, which
includes Sinasina, people live in scattered hamlets, with the
women's houses clustered around the men's house: the domestic
life of husband and wife would be geographically closer than
it is among Chimbu living west and south of the Chimbu River,
where the women's houses are more scattered. See also comments re division of labour on pp.

Table 9.2

Domestic work

Family	Household tasks*			Collecting and chopping firewood			Gardening			Totals		
	I**	C***	J≠	I	C	J	I	C	J	I	C	J
Social category I:												
A	4	-	-	1	-	-	-	1	-	5	1	-
B#	3	-	1	-	-	1	1	-	-	4	-	2
C	4	-	-	-	1	-	1	-	-	5	1	-
D	4	-	-	-	1	-	1	-	-	5	1	-
E	4	-	-	1	-	-	1	-	-	6	-	-
F#	4	-	-	1	-	-	1	-	-	6	-	-
G	4	-	-	1	-	-	none			5	-	-
H	4	-	-	1	-	-	none			5	-	-
I	4	-	-	1	-	-	1	-	-	6	-	-
J#	2	-	2	1	-	-	none			3	-	2
K#	4	-	-	1	-	-	1	-	-	6	-	-
L	4	-	-	1	-	-	1	-	-	6	-	-
M	4	-	-	1	-	-	1	-	-	6	-	-
Social category II:												
N	4	-	-	1	-	-	-	1	-	5	1	-
O	2	-	2	-	-	-	1	-	-	3	-	2
P	4##	-	-	1	-	-	-	1	-	5	1	-
Q	4	-	-	1	-	-	1	-	-	6	-	-
Social category III:												
R	2	-	2	none			-	1	-	2	1	2
S#	1	-	3	none			none			1	-	3
T	2	-	2	none			none			2	-	2

*   Cooking, washing-up, washing clothes, cleaning the house.

**   Independent activity.

*** Complementary activity.

≠   Joint activity.

\#   Wife working for money.

\#\# This husband said that when the children were younger he did domestic chores, but now he expected his daughter to help her mother.

Some Chimbu wives in Port Moresby considered that entertaining and being polite to their husbands' relatives and friends was part of a wife's marital duties. Others regarded it as one way a woman could help her husband, but not as a duty. To some extent the difference is probably a matter of degree. However, when does a wife's kindness to her husband's relatives surpass the demands of duty? How much does a husband expect of his wife? How much does society expect a wife to do as a duty? These are all very significant points in assessing the husband-wife relationship in any society but they are difficult to ascertain or measure. So often in social research it is the all-too-elusive overtones that are important in the analysis of social interaction.

In Table 9.2 assistance given regularly between a husband and wife appears as a joint activity. As noted in the table, husband P remarked that since his daughter was getting older (about eleven years) he now left it to her to help his wife. If this was common practice by Chimbu husbands, then obviously the stage of family development becomes a factor when organisation of domestic work is used to evaluate the degree of segregation of the conjugal role-relationship. It is also possible that the overall degree of segregation in the relationship may vary with the stage of development of the family.

Family A was the only other family in the sample with a daughter of an age that she was able to help her mother. However, husband A had never helped his wife with domestic tasks even when the children were young. Many more families would have to be studied before any conclusions could be reached about this point. Couples A and P were the two longest married couples in the sample.

Child care

Traditionally the husband, wife and several other relatives participate in child care. When her sons are about five, the mother has little say in their upbringing, and the father always has ultimate responsibility for the welfare of both his sons and daughters.

---

[1] As mentioned in Chapter 2, east of the Chimbu River, which includes Sinasina, people live in scattered hamlets, with the women's houses clustered around the men's house: the domestic life of husband and wife would be geographically closer than it is among Chimbu living west and south of the Chimbu River, where the women's houses are more scattered. See also comments re division of labour on pp.

Because of the paucity of tasks relating to child care in the category I and II families the organisation of parental activities in this regard was not assessed. The only assessment made, and I have doubts as to its validity as a criterion for assessing segregation in the husband-wife relationship, was whether the husband or wife said that the husband actively participated in the day-to-day care of their child or children, and if so, what form this participation took. This participation might be on a complementary or joint basis, but was seldom, if ever, on an independent basis. In the category I families it seldom involved more than playing with or watching a child while the mother was busy elsewhere or sleeping. For a few it meant carrying the child when the family went to the shops or to church. One of the category II fathers regularly bathed his daughter, played with her, and looked after her when his wife went to the pictures in the evenings. (They said some of the pictures frightened the child so they no longer took her.) By contrast, the category III parents, fathers and mothers, devoted much time and attention to their children, perhaps because of their diminished kinship ties. Fathers participated in child care more in categories II and III than in category I. In the latter, half the fathers did not participate in the care of their children beyond giving their wives money to buy food for the family. More family participation did not necessarily mean that there was more joint activity: the husband's participation might be complementary to that of the wife. In traditionally oriented families the father had the ultimate responsibility for the children and expected to make the decisions regarding them. In jointly organised child care, such as occurred in the two families with children in category III, the wife expected to have an equal share with her husband in decisions affecting their children; they regarded the children as belonging to both mother and father.

The number, age and sex[1] of children are all factors which may affect the amount of paternal participation in child care,

---

[1] These are important in Chimbu in determining which parent has the most contact with a child, but do not affect the conjugal role-relationship or ultimate control by the father of all unmarried children. Fathers have closer contact with their older sons, because they live in the same house. This seems to have produced little change in the system of control and care of children by husbands and wives in social categories I and II. However, particularly in social category II, but also in category I, kin participation in child care is reduced, particularly economic participation. Kinsmen in Port

but did not appear to be significant in the Chimbu families studied in Port Moresby. The amount of paternal participation in child care may be related to the total amount of child care activity performed by the parents. Maternal as well as paternal child activities were greater in category III families than in category I families. It could have been that the parent-child relationship, rather than the conjugal relationship, had become more joint, depending upon how paternal participation in child care was organised. This made comparison between the social categories difficult, because of the great difference in the number of child care activities between categories.

Bott (1971:22) mentions that London couples could not answer direct questions as to who was responsible for making decisions within the family. In traditional Chimbu society the norms of behaviour are specific, well known and almost inescapable for all due to the great interdependency of the members of a social group. In the domestic sphere, particularly in relation to child care, few conscious decisions need to be made by parents or by anyone else: things seemed to be done or not done almost automatically. The situation of rapid social change such as exists in Port Moresby called for an adaptation of the traditional system in this regard.

Husbands and wives who organised child care along traditional lines in Port Moresby mainly undertook complementary activities. When any problems arose, the husband was expected to make the decisions.[1] Whether he consulted with his wife, his kinsmen, or made an arbitrary decision, his wife had to carry it out. If she was not happy with the decision she would appeal to her husband's kinsmen. Her own kinsmen might support her if they felt she was not being well treated.[2]

---

1 (contd)
Moresby do come to see their nieces, nephews and young cousins, which establishes an interest - emotional and potentially economic - in them, even if they do not contribute actively to their welfare.

1 Sometimes he opted out and left the decision to the children themselves, but never, in my experience, did he ask his wife to make a decision in matters concerning children. If her husband was not present a wife would usually stall rather than make a decision regarding children (other than ones concerned with minor domestic matters).

2 Although after marriage a wife, for most social and economic purposes, belongs to her husband's patrilineage, her natal kin maintain interest in her and more particularly, have some

In the changed social environment in the town, conscious decisions regarding children had to be made from time to time because Chimbu social norms were not relevant to the urban environment. Such decisions were usually left to the children themselves, the father authorising the child to make the decision. There were no social norms concerning (i) whether a sick child should be taken to hospital; (ii) whether a child should go on to secondary school; (iii) whether, if a wife leaves her husband after a quarrel and returns to Chimbu, the children should remain in Port Moresby and finish their school-ing or return to Chimbu with their mother; and (iv) what to do if a child does not like washing or being washed.

Two of the category II families gave some thought to the care of their children, but in one case the children were still very young, and in the other case the two older children had been brought up by the husband's sister, and the parents saw very little of them. However, they maintained rights in the children by occasional gifts of clothes and food.

Leisure activities

In traditional Chimbu society, recreation is often one as-pect of activities which are held for other purposes, for example, dancing at pig festivals, speech-making and gesturing at food exchanges, singing at girls' puberty festivities, head-turning at courting parties. There is very little recreation for married women, although they may be required to partici-pate by cultivating or cooking extra food.

The activities used to assess the degree of segregation in leisure activities in Port Moresby were: going to Koke market (people go to the market as much to meet people as to buy things); going to church; visiting relatives or friends; gam-bling at home;[1] gambling away from home; watching or playing sport; going to the pictures; drinking at home; drinking away from home; going to committee meetings; going to a women's church group. These were the most frequent leisure-time activities, apart from simply sitting around talking. Some husbands and wives spent a considerable amount of time sitting in or just outside their houses, talking with each other

---

2 (contd)
rights and interests in her children. A husband's social group gives his wife's kinsmen a present a few weeks after the birth of each of her children, and they will give a share of the brideprice to the wife's kin when her daughters marry.

[1] Gambling is associated with card-playing.

together or with others. Sometimes men talked among themselves while women talked together, but as part of a single
group. Other husbands spent very little time at home.

It is difficult to assess sitting around talking in terms
of Bott's jointly and independently organised activities, and
to do this quantitatively would require measurements of the
time a husband and wife spent talking together with others,
in a sex-segregated group, and alone. Unfortunately I did not
keep such records.

Chimbu husbands in Port Moresby had more leisure-time occu-
pations than their wives, although this did not mean that they
had more leisure time. When women did take part in recreational activity other than simply talking to people, it was usually
with their husbands.

The sexual relationship

Bott (1971:83) states that families with loose-knit social
networks, which were also the ones with joint conjugal role-
relationships, placed considerable importance on the achieve-
ment of successful sexual relationships between husband and
wife, while families with segregated role-relationships did
not. Bott's information about the sexual relationships of
the couples in her sample was obtained at clinical interviews
conducted by the medical psycho-analyst. She mentions the
sexual relationship in her descriptions of the conjugal relationships of the families, but does not relate the information given to her classification of conjugal activities
according to independent, complimentary or joint organisation.

The term 'successful' in the context of the sexual relationship no doubt has different connotations for different couples,
whether Chimbu or London couples. I could not judge whether
the Chimbu couples I studied felt satisfied with their sexual
relationships. Sexual satisfaction did not appear to be very
significant part of the marriage relationship for Chimbu:[1] the
real importance of the sexual relationship of husband and wife
was that it was necessary for the procreation of children, and
it was important to a man that he have children.

The many traditional tabus against husbands and wives having sexual intercourse seemed to be still observed by Chimbu

---

[1] See pp.31, 32,33,40. One educated husband in my sample did
say that sex was important, but he did not necessarily mean
important in terms of a satisfying marital relationship.

Table 9.3

Abstinence from sexual intercourse*

	Social category I	Social category II	Social category III
No. of families	13	4	3
No. of couples abstaining	9	3	2**
Reasons given for abstaining:			
Wife breast-feeding	4***≠	2	1≠
Wife pregnant	2	0	0
Sleeping-room overcrowded	3	0	0
Wife old or sick	1	0	0
Did not want more children	1≠≠	0	2≠≠≠
No specific reason	0	1∅	0

* In some cases more than one reason applied to the same couple.

** One couple did not want to have any more children but I am not sure what, if any, steps they were taking to avoid the wife's becoming pregnant again. The husband said that the traditional method was to abstain from sexual relations, but he also said that his wife could go to the family planning clinic if she liked, but that he had no time to go.

*** A fifth woman was breast-feeding but she and her husband were not strictly observing the traditional custom of complete abstinence from sexual relations during this period.

≠ Includes two-year-old children pulling at their mother's breasts when upset, but they are not breast-feeding on a regular basis.

≠≠ Husband and wife did not agree about abstaining from sexual relations. The husband had to accede to his wife's wishes, and sexual intercourse was not, I was told, practised during the survey.

≠≠≠ One wife did in fact become pregnant when the survey ended.

∅ I think that this couple were simply following tradition by sleeping in different rooms. They had three children, the youngest being about six years old; the father appeared to be in his fifties and the mother in her thirties.

living in Port Moresby in 1972.[1] In addition, overcrowding
in houses caused some couples to abstain from sexual intercourse.

The fact that a high proportion of urban Chimbu couples
were apparently abstaining from sexual intercourse seems to
indicate that a close and 'successful' sexual relationship
was not important for these couples (see Table 9.3). According to Bott (1971:73, 83) such a situation would more likely
be found in segregated rather than joint conjugal relationships, and as we have seen, Chimbu conjugal relationships tend
to be highly segregated.

Possibly the nature of the sexual relationship of married
couples is a consequence of, rather than a facit in, the conjugal relationship, and that by its very nature it cannot be
classified as being independently, complementarily or jointly
organised. Certainly I am not able to make any such assessment from my information about the sexual practices and attitudes of Chimbu families.

---

[1] By 1973 tabus against sexual intercourse between men and
unmarried girls were slowly breaking down in Port Moresby,
especially among the younger men, due to the example of men
and women of other tribes.

Chapter 10

Quantitative analysis of conjugal relationships - attitudes

Introduction

The data in this chapter were collected from responses to
open-ended questions and from spontaneous remarks made during
general conversation. They concern attitudes about general
concepts that have some bearing on husband-wife relationships
or aspects of such concepts, rather than attitudes about the
organisation of activities. These attitudes are classified
as segregated, neutral or joint in nature according to whether
they are compatible with a joint or segregated conjugal role-
relationship or whether they are non-commital in this respect.

The characteristics of a good wife

The attitudes of husbands and wives were classified separately on the topic of what they thought were the characteristics of a good wife. There were twenty-nine different responses and these were grouped into segregated, neutral or
joint. Nearly all responses concerned the personal characteristics or behaviour of a wife, one major aspect relating to
economic activities and hard work, and the other to the personal relationships of the wife either within or outside the
family. These attitudes could readily be scaled on a continuum of the degree of segregation or jointness expressed in the
attitude. Those views expressing the importance of the wife
being good to people outside the nuclear family could be regarded as more segregated than those expressing the need for
a wife to be concerned with her nuclear family or with her
husband.

In traditional Chimbu society a wife is expected to maintain strong emotional ties with her natal group although for
most social purposes she acts as a member of her husband's
group which has legal, economic and procreative rights in her.
More stress is placed on a wife having successful relationships with her husband's kin group than on her getting on well
with her husband per se.

117

Table 10.1

Attitudes relating to a good wife*

Attitudes	Husbands' attitudes by social category			Wives' attitudes by social category		
	I	II	III	I	II	III
Segregated:						
1. Obedient	B,C,D,I	N,O		D,E,H,L	N,Q	
2. Economic and hardworking	A,C,D,E, H,J,K,L	O,P		C,D,H,K, M	Q	
3. Works for money if she has no small children	D	Q		D,H		
4. Stresses relationships with her own or her husband's kin group	B,D,J,M	Q	R,S	C,M	O,P	S
Neutral:**						
5. Has children but not too many	L			A,L		
6. Must not get angry with her husband	B,C,H,J	O	R	B,H,J		
Joint:						
7. Does not flirt	A,J	P		M		
8. Intrafamilial relationships stressed			S	D		R,S
9. Good-looking, intelligent			T			

* No information from wife T and couples F, G and I. Husband R (category III) said that a good wife should take part in community affairs. Husband I (category I) said that he did not know the attributes of a good wife because he left Chimbu when he was a small boy and came to Port Moresby.

** Neutral in regard to conjugal role segregation as they either bear no relation to it (no.5) or I was unable to interpret the response in terms of conjugal role segregation (no.6).

Attitudes emphasising the importance of the economic contribution of the wife are regarded as segregational in nature,
as economic activities in traditional Chimbu society are organised on a complementary or independent basis. In Table 10.1
people's views are classified according to their degree of
segregation on the basis of a subjective and speculative assessment.

Obedience and economic activities and not getting angry
with one's husband were mentioned most frequently by both husbands and wives as the characteristics of a good wife. These
opinions may be exaggerated because there were more families
in social category I than in the other two categories and few
of them had views classified as joint. Equal numbers of families in each category might have produced a different overall
impression.[1]

The characteristics of
a good husband

Table 10.2 lists husbands' and wives' views on which attributes are important in defining a good husband. I have classified 'does not drink' and 'does not gamble' as neutral because,
although Chimbu living in Port Moresby would primarily object
to these activities on economic grounds they could also have
social or religious objections to these practices, or resent
the amount of time spent on these activities rather than being
spent on family activities.

The overall pattern of the responses is similar to that of
Table 10.1, there being slightly fewer husbands who stressed
that good husbands should not fight with their wives than
there had been husbands saying that a good wife should not
fight with her husband. More wives suggested that a good husband should not fight with his wife than suggested a good wife
should not quarrel with her husband. Little emphasis was giv-
en to a husband's being obedient to his wife. Factors concerned with economic production were the characteristics most
frequently mentioned as being desirable in a husband. There
is no apparent pattern of different attitudes in the various
categories.

Why do people marry?

A number of Chimbu husbands and wives found this question
difficult either to understand or to answer, perhaps because

---

[1] The comment made by husband I (see Table 10.1) indicates that
the responses made may refer to social norms rather than to individual opinions. However, in tribal societies social and
individual attitudes tend to coincide more than is the case in
industrialised societies.

Table 10.2

Attitudes relating to a good husband*

Attitudes	Husbands' attitudes by social category			Wives' attitudes by social category		
	I	II	III	I	II	III
Segregated:						
1. Obedient				M	Q	T
2. Works hard, is good in business, gives money to wife and kin	A,C,D, H,J	P,Q	R,T	C,D,H, J,K,M		
3. Gives plenty of things to wife and her kin	A,F	N,Q		D,F,K	O,Q	
Neutral:						
4. Does not gamble or drink	A**			C,D	N	
5. Does not have children too close together				L		
6. Friendly to everyone					S	
7. Does not fight or argue with wife.	H	O		E,H,J, K,M	P	
Joint:						
8. Does not flirt	C,G			G		
9. Intrafamilial relationships stressed	I	P,Q	R	E,H,M	P	
10. Helps wife	I	O	R	H,M		S

* No information from husbands B,E,K,L,M and S, and wives A,B,I and J.

** Drinking only not good.

of their lack of conceptual thinking and because of the auto-
maticity of most social processes in traditional Chimbu society.
Some respondents gave more than one reason.

Several people cited parents or relatives as instigating
the formalities of marriage, but only after a man and woman
had already become attracted to each other and the woman had
let it be known that she would like to marry the man. Probably mutual attraction between spouses was often a factor in
initiating formal marriage arrangements by the couple's respective kin, although this certainly was not always the case.

Owing to the small number of responses that could be tabulated, Table 10.3 does not provide sufficient information to
indicate characteristics of jointness or segregation in the
expectations of marriage relationships in the families studied.
None of the reasons for marriage indicate that a joint conjugal relationship was expected, but this may be in part because the couples had in mind the formalities of the marriage
'ceremony' as distinct from ideas about the two individuals
being married. They were thinking of marriage in social terms
rather than in terms of the two individuals concerned, because
for the Chimbu, marriage formalities are a social aspect of
the conjugal relationship, marriage as an institution having
both individual and social implications.

One of the difficulties in quantifying social research data
is that many of the overtones and implications of information
given by respondents may be lost. In trying to include these
overtones the tabulation may become cumbersome. For example,
in attitude 6 I try to indicate that although some of the informants said that people married because their parents wished
it, and that the parents probably wished it to obtain brideprice for their daughter or to establish friendly relationships with the prospective spouse's kin group,[1] in many instances the parents would only be willing to marry their
daughter to someone the girl herself wished to marry.[2] But

---

[1] An automatic consequence of brideprice payments and marriage
exchanges.

[2] Reasons why a boy or girl want to marry each other were not
given, but the existence of mutual attraction between them
was often implied. One husband noted that many young Chimbu
girls were now marrying older men who had been successful in
business. He implied that the girls wanted the 'good things
of life'. Another cause of this phenomenon might be that in
recent years there are fewer young men in many parts of Chimbu
because they are away living in towns or working on plantations.
However, in a society where polygyny is practised it is likely

Table 10.3

Attitudes to why people marry*

Attitudes	Husbands' attitudes by social category			Wives' attitudes by social category		
	I	II	III	I	II	III
Segregated:						
1. For economic or domestic services	A,G,K				E,G	
2. For sexual services			S			S
3. Because daughter wishes to get brideprice for parents	A					
4. Because relatives wish it	C				P	
5. Parents wish it because a European may have persuaded them to let their daughter marry him	A					
Neutral:						
6. Parents wish it after boy and girl attracted to each other	B				B,C	
(i) to get brideprice	A		N			N
(ii) because they are afraid their daughter will become pregnant	A					
7. To have children	G,K		S	G		S
8. It is God's plan			S			S
9. To get away from a previous husband	A					

* No information from husbands E and P, wives A and K, and couples D,F,H,I,J,L,M,O, Q,R and T.

here again motives may be mixed. They will want their daughter to be happy for her own sake, but at the same time realise that if she is not happy she may run away and brideprice may have to be returned or bad relationships may develop between their social group and that of their son-in-law.

The first five attitudes in Table 10.3 are interpreted as expressing a segregated view of the conjugal relationship; the remainder do not imply segregation in the marriage relationship, except perhaps the view that people marry to have children, but neither do they indicate a joint conjugal relationship. None of the reasons given for people marrying seemed to indicate the expectation of a joint husband-wife relationship in marriage.

'Why do many husbands leave their wives in Chimbu when they are in Port Moresby?'

The replies to this question are tabulated in Table 10.4. Nearly all responses stressed the importance of economic factors rather than emotional ties in the conjugal relationship, apart from the sentiment that the husband may not like his wife and would therefore leave her in Chimbu. Respondents may have assumed that in cases where the wife remained in Chimbu there was no emotional tie between husband and wife, but this was not mentioned. If a wife's remaining in Chimbu did indicate a lack of emotional ties between spouses, then, as such a high proportion of wives remained in Chimbu, emotional ties between spouses would not appear to be a norm in Chimbu conjugal relationships. Again, if joint relationships were the norm there would probably have been more responses relating to the husband's not liking the wife as a reason for leaving her in Chimbu, and a lower proportion mentioning economic considerations only. From the responses given, it would seem that economic factors had priority over social, sexual, procreative or emotional factors in Chimbu conjugal relationships.

It is difficult to arrange the views given according to their implication as to the degree of conjugal role-segregation. Six of the replies indicated that the decision as to whether the wife came to Port Moresby was more likely to lie with the husband than with the wife, and gave economic, social or emotional reasons why the husband might not want to have his

---

2 (contd)
that there was always a proportion of young girls married to older men. Since the completion of the study a number of other Chimbu have noted this same phenomenon.

Table 10.4

Attitudes to husbands leaving wives in Chimbu during their long-term residence in Port Moresby*

Attitudes	Husbands' attitudes by social category			Wives' attitudes by social category		
	I	II	III	I	II	III
Segregated:						
1. Wife doesn't want to come to Port Moresby	C				P	
2. Husband doesn't want to spend money on her (various reasons)	A	N,P		E,G		S
3. Husband cannot afford her in town (i.e., husband unemployed)	B,J			B,D,		
4. Why not? It is alright				H		
5. Husband doesn't send money for her fare					N	
6. Husband wants her to grow coffee				D,E		S
7. Wife wants to grow coffee	C			E,H		
8. Husband wants her to look after his relatives				E	N	
Neutral:						
9. Husband doesn't like her			R	G,I,L		

* No information from husbands D,E,G,H,I,L,S, wives A,C,J,R, and couples F,K,M,O,Q,T.

wife in Port Moresby (attitudes 2,5,6,7,8,9). Attitude 1 does
not suggest any reason why the wife might not want to come to
Port Moresby, but wife P, in addition to suggesting that a
wife might not want to come to Port Moresby, indicated that
a wife might prefer to stay in the Chimbu and grow coffee, so
that this may more accurately be regarded as the same reply
as attitude 6.

No trends except the importance of economic factors show
up in Table 10.4, perhaps because of the small numbers involved. During discussions only family P, in category II,
said that they thought that it was bad for husbands and wives
to be separated for any length of time. Wife S in category
III said that she would always go wherever her husband went.
If a companionate type of marriage with a joint conjugal relationship was the norm in Chimbu society, then it would be
likely that wives would express the undesirability of long
periods of physical separation of husbands and wives, or a
larger proportion of respondents would have suggested reasons
outside of the control of the individuals concerned (e.g. an
inadequate income or lack of accommodation in town) as the
cause of wives remaining in Chimbu. The question then would
be: why does the husband come to Port Moresby? If the conjugal relationship was joint it would be unlikely that he
would stay in the city by himself for any length of time.
Family P suggested that it was bad for a husband and wife to
be separated because the wife might find herself another
husband; this does not necessarily imply an expectation of a
joint conjugal role-relationship in marriage.

Attitudes to husbands and wives
sleeping in the same house

The husband and wife in all families studied lived and
slept in the same house,[1] except for family O.[2] In several
homes husband and wife did not sleep in the same room, and in
others they slept in separate beds or on separate mats.[3]

---

[1] No provision was made for men's houses in the low-cost housing suburbs. In the shanty settlements there were several
men's 'dormitories' but these were very overcrowded. Husbands
with wives in Port Moresby did not usually sleep in these
dormitories.

[2] During the first part of the research period, couple O did
not have their own house; the wife, but not the husband, was
permitted to stay with relatives in an army compound. This
separation was not their own choice.

[3] In many Papua New Guinean tribes sexual intercourse, marital
or otherwise, usually takes place in the bush or gardens.

Table 10.5

Attitudes to husbands sleeping in men's houses*

Attitudes	Husbands' attitudes by social category			Wives' attitudes by social category		
	I	II	III	I	II	III
Segregated:						
1. Prefers separate houses for husband and wife	B,D, G,J			A,B,C,D, E,G,H,J		
2. In Port Moresby husband must look after wife at night**	A,H			A,B,I,K		
Neutral:						
3. Indifferent					Q	
4. Likes one house in Port Moresby and separate houses in Chimbu	A,F,H	N		F,I,K,L	N,P	
Joint:						
5. Prefers one house for husband and wife together	C,L	P	S,T			R,S, T***

* No information from husbands E,I,K,Q,R and couples M and O.

** The husbands and wives who mentioned this preferred separate houses but realised this might not be practical in Port Moresby.

*** Wife R said that when they go to Chimbu on holiday, she doesn't mind whether her husband sleeps with her or in the men's house.

Nearly all the category I families preferred that men live in men's houses and women in their own individual houses, but because they were afraid of prowlers in Port Moresby they felt husbands should sleep in the same house as their wives in order to protect them. Wives said that they did not want their husbands around all the time, especially when they were cooking. One husband said that the advantage of a husband and wife having separate houses was that if some small quarrel developed between them then the husband could go off to the men's house and tempers had time to cool off before the husband and wife came in contact again.

None of the category II or III families preferred separate houses for husbands and wives in Port Moresby; all those in category III preferred to have one house in both Port Moresby and Chimbu. Preference for a single house for the nuclear family was a more joint attitude towards the husband-wife relationship than preference for men to live in men's houses and women to live in their own houses.

Attitudes to polygyny

Bott studied the conjugal relationships and social networks of monogamous families who lived in a society where polygyny had been illegal for hundreds of years. By contrast, in 7 of the 20 Chimbu families studied, husbands (all in social category I) either were or had been polygynists. One man said that one wife was enough for any man while other husbands would be happy to become polygynists should the need or the occasion arise. Some wives would have accepted a co-wife, without argument, in certain circumstances.

In Chimbu, as in Papua New Guinea in general, polygyny was not widely practised but most men considered it the ideal form of marriage. Christian missionaries strongly condemned the practice, but even strong adherents of the church sometimes said they could not understand why a husband with more than one wife was not allowed to become a member of the church.

Although the church's influence may have reduced the incidence of polygyny in the Chimbu, it did not succeed in breaking down the traditional attitude of segregation in the marriage relationship and replacing it with the more joint attitudes and practices recommended by the modern church. People who would not practise polygyny for Christian reasons were still able to appreciate its value in particular situations, and some found it difficult to understand the Christian ruling on polygyny. Even among Christians the traditional attitudes may not have changed, but their practices in this regard had.

Table 10.6

Attitudes to polygyny*

Attitudes	Husbands attitudes by social category			Wives' attitudes by social category		
	I	II	III	I	II	III
Segregated						
1. Polygyny is good	B,C,G,H, I,J,L,M	Q				S
2. Polygyny good in certain circumstances:						
(i) if first wife barren	H,K			H,M		S
(ii) if first wife doesn't want any more children				L		
(iii) if first wife old and sick				A,J		
Neutral:						
3. Polygyny is alright - it is up to the husband but first wife must agree	A	N		A,J	N,O	
4. Polygyny is necessary if first wife has only daughters		Q				
5. Polygyny is alright in Chimbu but not in Port Moresby for economic reasons	D,I,J	P	R,S,T			
6. One wife is enough	F	P		D,E,H,K	P	R,T
7. Polygyny is alright for others but not for me or my spouse			R	B,C	Q	S
8. Does not know				F		
9. It is old-fashioned but not bad			T	I		
10. It is un-Christian**	D,G,H,L	Q	S	C,L		S,T
Possibly joint:						
11. It is bad. It leads to quarrels due to jealousy				G		

---

* No information for husbands E and O. Husband A said that it was up to the husband whether he wanted to have more than one wife. He said most of the older men favoured polygyny, but the younger men influenced by the missions thought they would only have one wife. Wife G said that it was too much work for the husband to prepare gardens for more than one wife, and this would lead to quarrels.

** This view does not imply a condemnation of polygyny or polygynists because even for Christians traditional views persisted.

Economic factors might also have affected their practice, as
particularly in the urban situation, a wife tends to be an
economic liability rather than an asset.

Table 10.6 shows that more husbands than wives considered
polygyny to be positively good. Only one person, a wife, said
that polygyny was unconditionally bad. A positive view of
polygyny may indicate an expectation that the conjugal role-
relationship will be segregated rather than joint. Most of
the views expressed seemed to be pragmatic rather than senti-
mental or related to emotional ties between husband and wife.
Category III families may be less in favour of polygyny than
the families in other social categories, and category III
wives might be the strongest opponents if their husbands
wished to become polygynists.

Attitudes to supernatural powers

Many Chimbu said that witchcraft (<u>sanguma</u>) was prevalent
in the Chimbu and most believed that some people were possessed by superhuman, uncontrollable evil powers that would be
vent upon kinsfolk or affines if they were in any way offended
by them.[1] The significance of the belief for this study is
that it served to maintain kinship ties and the giving and receiving of services between kinsmen and affines, thereby reducing or making difficult close ties within the nuclear family for there is a limit to the number of social ties to which
an individual can be committed.

Sometimes Chimbu families in Port Moresby were without food
or money only two days after pay-day. Apart from drinking and
gambling, the husband's income was frequently given to a kinsman to help pay a court fine, to buy a plane ticket back to
Chimbu or for some traditional purpose. If I inquired why the
husband had not kept part of his pay to buy food for his family, the reply would be, 'But the man was my brother!' or 'The
man was my uncle!'. In situations such as these it is very
difficult to evaluate motives. Did the donor act from affection or from fear? However, whichever it be, there was always
the knowledge that sometime, somewhere, the equivalent of that
which was given would be returned by the receiver or by one of
his kinsmen.

---

[1] I have already mentioned the case of the husband and wife
who both wanted the wife to have an operation, but because the
wife's parents objected the couple reluctantly cancelled the
operation. The husband was afraid that when they returned to
the Chimbu his in-laws might kill him through witchcraft if
he allowed his wife to have the operation.

Table 10.7 shows that most people in the sample believed that sanguma was an active force in Chimbu but they were not sure whether it existed in Port Moresby. Sanguma is believed to act between people who are related by blood or marriage so they were not concerned about the practices of non-Chimbus living in Port Moresby;[1] as one Chimbu pointed out, they did not speak these people's languages so it was unlikely that they knew about their practices. Belief in sanguma is a form of social control which reinforces kinship ties but not the conjugal tie. Husbands and wives do not settle disputes between each other by resorting to this means, so it does not sanction their behaviour towards each other. By reinforcing kinship and affinal ties, belief in witchcraft indirectly emphasises segregation rather than jointness in the conjugal relationship. Those people who believed that sanguma was a force in the Chimbu but not in Port Moresby still had to be careful to meet their obligations to kin and affines when they were in Port Moresby because if they did not, they might be affected by witches on their return to Chimbu.[2]

Table 10.7 shows that husbands in social categories II and III were the people most likely not to believe in witchcraft. Three of these men claimed that they were not interested in maintaining relationships with all their kin and did not give money to everyone who asked. Husband P, who evicted his relatives from his house, said that he would spend the rest of his life in Port Moresby and that there were no people in the city who could harm him or his wife by means of witchcraft or sorcery.[3]

Views on changes in the division of labour in Port Moresby[4]

In many of the families studied the husband worked hard to earn money while his wife had little to do at home. Frequently

---

[1] Anthropologists who have studied witchcraft accusations in African societies state that such accusations commonly occur between co-wives and close kinsmen, but do not usually mention affines (see Marwick (1965) and Nadel (1952)).

[2] Husband D claimed that he would not go back to Chimbu to live because he was afraid that sanguma would attack his children.

[3] The churches taught that witchcraft was not a real force, but it was the hospital (sanguma usually manifested itself by suddenly causing illness and frequently death) rather than Christian teachings that seemed to be undermining belief in witchcraft in Port Moresby among social category I families.

[4] See Appendix B for a summary of the traditional Chimbu division of labour.

Table 10.7

Attitudes to witchcraft*

Attitudes	Husbands' attitudes, by social category			Wives' attitudes, by social category		
	I	II	III	I	II	III
Reflecting belief in witchcraft:						
1. Knows someone in Port Moresby possessed by sanguma	L			L		
2. Believes sanguma exists in Port Moresby and in Chimbu	C,H			A,H		R,T
3. Believes sanguma exists in Chimbu but doesn't know about Port Moresby	A,F,J,K			C,E,F, J,K	N,Q	
4. Believes sanguma exists in Chimbu but not in Port Moresby	B,D	O,P		B,D,M	O,P***	
5. Possibly sanguma in Chimbu but definitely not in Port Moresby			S			
6. Does not know whether sanguma exists	I					S
Reflecting disbelief in witchcraft:						
7. Does not believe in sanguma because has not seen proof of it		N,**Q	R,T	I		

* No information from husbands E and M and couple G.

** Husband N said that he did not believe in sanguma because he was a Christian. He said that the modern form of 'love magic' practised in Port Moresby was to have nice clothes and a good job.

*** Wife P said that there was no sanguma in Port Moresby because the government was there. It was not clear what she meant by this, i.e., were witches afraid of the government, or did the government perform the functions of witches, that is punish people who committed social offences so that there was, as it were, no need for witches to function?

unemployed kinsmen of the husband or the wife could assist her if she needed it. Consequently most husbands did not feel called upon to help with domestic tasks. This situation in itself may tend towards segregation in the conjugal role-relationship with regard to activities, but it might not be an index of the husband's attitudes towards his own wife or of ties of sentiment towards her, or of his views on the roles of husband and wife. Behaviour is regulated to a large extent by felt needs, in a particular situation as well as by the norms of society.

Table 10.8 shows the different attitudes between families in social categories I and III. The category I families lived in different types of household arrangements to those they were brought up in, but their attitudes and practices regarding the division of labour between spouses did not seem to have changed.[1] Owing to circumstances outside their control, many wives were unable to participate in economic production or earning in Port Moresby. The views expressed indicate that category I and II families were more likely to have segregated conjugal role-relationships than category III families.

In Table 10.8, views 1 and 2 reveal expectations of segregation in marital roles of Chimbu families in Port Moresby. View 3 is more neutral, recognising that there is the possibility of individual variation from the normal segregated pattern. View 4 is an expression of there being less segregation, or more jointness, in conjugal relationships in Port Moresby.

Discussion of findings relating
to attitudes

In almost all cases there were more segregated activities and attitudes than there were joint ones. In some instances this reflected the larger number of families in social category I (e.g., Table 10.5 and 10.8) where attitudes tended to vary according to social category. In other cases (e.g., Tables 10.1 and 10.2) segregated and joint views occurred in all categories and the fact that more segregated than joint views were expressed probably indicated that husband-wife relationships among Chimbu were more segregated than joint in nature.

---

[1] With the possible exception of couple J, attitudes expressed here reflect how the couples behaved, or would like to behave, i.e., wives would like to have participated in economic activities or to have had gardens in Port Moresby as they did in Chimbu.

Table 10.8

**Attitudes to division of labour between
husband and wife in Port Moresby***

Attitudes	Husbands' attitudes, by social category			Wives' attitudes, by social category		
	I	II	III	I	II	III
Expect segregated activities:						
1. Less segregation of activities in Chimbu	A,C,H,K	N,O		A,C,H,K	O	
2. Division of labour basically the same in Chimbu and Port Moresby	B,D,F, G,I,J,** L	P		B,E,F, I,J,L, M	P	
Neutral:						
3. It is regulated by individual choice	G***	O		G***	O	
Expect less segregation:						
4. There is less segregation in the division of labour in Port Moresby			R,S,T	D		R,S,T

---

*   No information for husbands E and M, wife N and couple Q.

**   Husband J said he helped his wife more in Port Moresby because she was working for money.

*** Couple G said that the division of labour between husband and wife was basically the same in Chimbu and Port Moresby, and that husband G always helped his wife a great deal in both places; they conceded that other husbands might not behave this way but that was up to them, i.e., there is opportunity for individual choice in this regard. See p.108 for a discussion on the difficulties of determining when an activity is performed on a joint basis, due to a social norm, and when it is performed on the basis of an individual spouse assisting the other spouse.

The data gained from this exploratory study indicate possible trends in family relationships and the difficulties involved in studying such relationships. The difficulties encountered in trying to quantify and tabulate the data show some of the problems which would be involved in a large-scale study of tribal families living in an urban environment. However, the attempt at quantitative analysis was of value in that it focused on specific details which are significant in understanding family relationship but which might be overlooked or given insufficient attention in a qualitative analysis. They also help to clarify the distinction between actual behaviour and attitudes or social norms.

Chapter 11

Summary and conclusions

Introduction

Although this study is based on a small sample of urban
Chimbu families, it provides an indication of what to expect
in such families and, when looked at against the background
of rural, traditional family organisation and relationships,
suggests the types of change and continuity occurring among
Chimbu families of differing social and economic backgrounds.
With one exception, all the husbands and wives were born in
the highlands, and of these only one was born outside Chimbu.
But the proportion of their lives spent in Chimbu, in school
and/or boarding school, and the attitudes of their parents
and relatives to the social, economic and religious changes
that were introduced to the Chimbu since the arrival of Europeans, varied greatly.

Rural family relationships

The traditional husband-wife relationship is highly segregated, work being clearly divided into men's work and women's
work.[1] Husbands have their family responsibilities and activities, which they organise in consultation with other men in the
men's house rather than with their wives, who live in houses
separate from their husbands. Wives carry out their domestic
and gardening activities independently but rely on their husbands to clear the land before gardening. Wives look after
pigs and young children under the direction of their husbands
but without day-to-day supervision or consultation.

From the point of view of the husband and wife, the conjugal relationship is primarily economic and procreative. The
nuclear family is the basic unit in economic production, and
the presence of children, who socially, and in Chimbu belief
biologically, belong only to their father, often binds a marriage together when otherwise the husband and wife might

---

[1] See Appendix B.

separate. While many marriages result from the mutual attraction of a boy and girl, others are arranged by parents or kin for socio-political or economic reasons. Any strong emotional involvement between husband and wife is tempered by the traditional antagonism and fear that exists between people of opposite sexes; social limitations are placed on sexual and social intercourse between husbands and wives, and for men all sexual intercourse becomes a somewhat hazardous activity.

Marriage gives status to a man, and polygyny gives even greater status, although few men were and are able to achieve the ideal of more than one wife. Marriage also provides men with the children which they all desire.[1] The benefits to a woman of marriage are mainly economic: someone to make a house for her, to break in new garden land and build fences for her; it may mean an increase in her pig herd. It also provides her with the means, in the form of brideprice, to make her parents happy. At the same time it usually causes both the bride and her parents some unhappiness because she goes to live with strangers, her husband's parents and kin.

Although traditionally there is a very sharp division of labour between husband and wife there are also institutionalised ways for spouses to help each other if they wish. Carrying water and cooking (except of pigs, chickens and a certain type of pandanus nut which is highly prized among the Chimbu) are considered to be women's work, but some husbands occasionally chose to help their wives with these things. Society does not condemn spouses who do not help in such ways but does condemn a husband or wife who does not perform his or her respective duties according to the norms of society.

Marriage in Chimbu also has important social implications for the respective kin groups of the couple. Once a boy and girl are married their kin groups are linked in a friendly relationship which manifests itself in economic, ritual, social and political bonds and ties of reciprocity. Thus these groups have an interest in maintaining successful marriages and in this context the husband-wife relationship acts as a single, combined unit within the kin group of the husband. In Bott's terms, the family is encapsulated within the kin group of the husband. But the Chimbu wife maintains strong emotional ties with her natal group and visits them regularly; some of her kin also occasionally visit her, and maintain an interest in her children, particularly her daughters.

---

[1] Traditionally if a wife does not have children, she and her husband will separate or he will take a second wife.

Chimbu society is patrilineal. Fathers and their kinsmen
have authority over children and make all the important decisions regarding their up-bringing. The mother simply looks
after the children when they are small and provides food for
them until they are married. However, the up-bringing of
children is rather a casual business and kinsmen as well as
parents contribute towards their care.[1] This may give kinsmen the right to a say in a girl's marriage arrangements, or
a direct claim on a portion of the brideprice.

The social categories

Although the three social categories into which the twenty
urban Chimbu families were classified were based on a subjective assessment of life-style and were difficult to define,
their use was justified because some distinct differences in
husband-wife relationships and the social networks of the
families in the three categories were detected. There was a
much greater distinction in the patterns of living of families
in social categories II and III than there was between those
in categories I and II. This may simply have been the result
of the small sample, and in fact there may be families whose
husband-wife relationship and social network composition and
degree of connectedness is intermediate between those of families in my sample in categories II and III. Social relationships between families of different life-styles sometimes cut
across the hypothetical divisions of the social categories,
due to the strength of kinship ties and the essentially egalitarian nature of traditional Chimbu society, but such inter-
category relationships were limited. Until Chimbu husbands
and wives have lived outside the Chimbu for some years and
have sufficient education to enable them to take up semi-
skilled or clerical work in Port Moresby, it is unlikely that
there will be families to bridge the present sharp division
between social category II and III families.

Social category I families

The domestic activities and social networks of these families were very similar in most respects to those of families in

---

[1] This does not mean that emotional ties do not develop between
a mother and children, particularly her daughters. Older
daughters may have very little direct contact with their fathers.
Moreover, emotional as well as social interaction involves a
larger number of people than would the case with the children
of most Western families, and from an early age children begin
to appreciate the importance of group membership.

the Chimbu. Husbands and wives were forced by circumstances and/or the need to protect women in the urban situation, to live and sleep in the same house, usually with other Chimbu families from the same area or with single men related to one of the spouses.[1] However, this did not necessarily mean that a more joint relationship developed between husband and wife; in fact, this close proximity might be a source of tension and irritability between them.

Many of the husbands lived in Port Moresby for many years before marrying or before their wives (and children) came to the city. During this period they usually spent much time and money gambling and drinking, a pattern of living which they saw no reason to change when their wives and families arrived.[2] Kinsmen and others from the same part of the Chimbu were the main drinking and gambling companions as well as being the people who would help them in times of trouble (e.g., bail them out of gaol, feed them when unemployed). Some families had a close social network comprised of Chimbu who attended the same church. These relationships were based on social group membership in a similar way that social relationships in the Chimbu were based on a man's membership of a kin group.

Many Chimbu men in Port Moresby had individual relationships with work-mates, past work-mates, or more rarely with Papuans who adopted them when they came to Port Moresby as boys. Such relationships were similar to the trade-partner

---

[1] More recently an increasing number of single girls and barren women have come to live in Port Moresby, having heard of the exciting and comfortable life in the city and the lucrative business of prostitution. Some parents did not wish their daughters to participate in this business while others were in favour. But in a society where the male-female relationship is basically an economic one, where economic motivation is strong in all spheres of life, sanctions against this new form of business - against which there are no specific traditional sanctions because traditionally prostitution was not practised - are not very strong. Some of the men in town had heard about venereal disease, but the girls seemed to understand very little about these types of disease.

[2] It may be that Chimbu men were escaping from an unpleasant situation through their heavy drinking; another factor producing heavy drinking may have been that the buying of drinks for kin and friends had taken the place of some traditional food and gift displays and exchanges.

relationships of men in the Chimbu, being both social and economic in content; for example, kampani members, drinking partners, and gambling partners.[1]

The lot of the wives in Port Moresby, many of whom came to town of their own accord,[2] was much less satisfactory than that of the husbands, particularly if they had no brothers or close male relatives to guard their interests and provide emotional support. Only a few obtained paid employment; the others were completely dependent upon their husbands for economic support in a manner that never existed in Chimbu. This reduced their status in the husband-wife relationship. If her husband was irresponsible there was very little that a wife could do about it particularly if she had no kinsmen in Port Moresby or if the dispute occurred in a non-traditional context or was a consequence of the new set of circumstances in the urban situation. For example, a man who gave his pay to a close kinsman rather than to his wife to buy food for their family may not be condemned by other Chimbu. In the Chimbu a wife always has the food she grows in her garden, unless she herself has neglected her duties, so the Chimbu in Port Moresby had no institutionalised attitude of condemning a man who did not provide money for food. In Chimbu if a husband did not provide for his wife on a long-term basis the wife might return to her own kin, the traditional method solving such a problem. She would do this by her own means and no doubt with the approval of her kinsmen. However, in Port Moresby she would need a plane fare to do this, and in one particular case at the time of my study, no one was prepared to provide the women with the fare.[3] Instead, a kinsman of the husband convened a prayer meeting to ask God to prevail on the husband to change his ways. Whether new methods to

---

[1] Winnings were shared if one gambled with kin. With non-kin, and more particularly non-Chimbu, the relationship was purely economic and a man kept his winnings himself.

[2] The case-histories in Appendix C give some of the reasons for wives coming to Port Moresby, sometimes after several years of separation from their husbands: tales about the good things of Port Moresby, the drop in the price of coffee, boredom in Chimbu, etc., motivated them to come to the city.

[3] A consequence largely of a belief that it would be against Christian teaching to facilitate the separation of husband and wife.

solve problems in the urban situation which cannot be solved by traditional methods finally become institutionalised will depend, at least in part, upon whether they prove to be effective in the early cases.[1]

In the Chimbu there is no need for a husband to give his wife the equivalent of a personal allowance. She makes her own attire from raw materials she can acquire herself and through their combined efforts the food for social events is produced. He is expected to give presents to her family. Some of the couples in social category I did give presents to the wife's relatives in Port Moresby or sent money to her relatives in Chimbu which was probably the closest thing to a wife's allowance that these husbands provided. They believed that they adequately fulfilled their duties as husbands by giving their wives some kind of roof over their heads and $2 a fortnight to buy food for the household. Sometimes this was supplemented by other people living in the house, sometimes not.

Marital quarrels sometimes developed because wives, bored with no land to garden and finding the climate too hot to walk around with small children, spent their time, and sometimes their food money, gambling. A husband would complain that his wife had wasted the food money he had given her. A wife's duties in Port Moresby were limited: cooking the food and possibly buying some of it; washing the few clothes that the family possessed; sweeping out the house and the ground around it; and caring for small children, which required very little effort as traditional Chimbu methods were followed by all but social category III families. Working wives were in a better position than those who were not working, because they had young children or because they had no skills needed in Port Moresby. As occurred traditionally, a working wife in Port Moresby controlled her own earnings, having money to buy clothes, betel nut and cigarettes for herself and to gamble if she wished, as well as to give presents to her kinsmen. But probably most important, she had a profitable way of spending her time and occupying her mind. Consequently she was a much happier person than the unemployed, unsophisticated wife. Her husband was happier too because their partnership was more like the traditional one he was brought up to expect: an

---

[1] Neither church nor government welfare services were seen as a means of resolving family problems in Port Moresby. None of the families studied had any experience of government services or saw such services as a function of the church to which they belonged. Traditional methods were recognised, but sometimes they were not available or did not meet the needs of the urban situation.

economically productive partnership which provided opportunities for gift-exchanges with the kinsmen of both husband and
wife.

For the husband whose wife was unable to work there seemed
few advantages in having her in Port Moresby. She cooked for
him and might wash his clothes, but during the years he was in
the city on his own he probably found it satisfactory cooking
with other 'single' men and doing his own washing. Sexual
services were of limited importance, partly due to traditional
values, and partly because of tabus associated with sexual
intercourse during pregnancy or lactation.[1] Wives tended to
be a liability both economically and because of the crowded
conditions and dangers of urban life, particularly at night.
Having children and the company of one's own children was
important, but some men were content if these were in Chimbu;
others might bring a son to Port Moresby to keep him company
while his wife and daughters remained in Chimbu, perhaps looking after his coffee garden. Other men preferred to have their
children in Port Moresby either because they had transgressed
some traditional obligations and were afraid their children
might be harmed by witchcraft, or because they considered that
schools in Port Moresby were better than those in Chimbu, that
their children would learn better English in town and therefore obtain better jobs and have more economic assets with
which to look after their father when he became too old to
work. If a man had a number of children in town then he needed
his wife to look after them.

Parents in social categories I and II seemed unaware of
their inadequacies in preparing their children for a new way
of life. Almost unconsciously they expected the school to do
this for them because they thought that the only real difference between their way of life and that of their children when
they grow up was that the latter, as a result of education,
would be able to earn more money and have more of the things
at present associated with the white man. They did not anticipate changes in social or other aspects of life nor understand
how to train their children for urban life; the new way of
resolving problems in the town was to let the children themselves make the day-to-day decisions. Parents were not aware
of the long-term problems being created nor of the consequences

---

[1] Prostitutes were available in town but I do not know whether
many Chimbu men had used their services in the past. It seems
unlikely, because of the strength until recently of traditional
beliefs among the uneducated in regard to sexual practices, and
because, until recently, most prostitutes were Papuan women.

of the present situation. They did not anticipate problems arising between themselves and children as the latter became older. This situation was aggravated by the casual tradition-al system of training children and because not only parents but kinsmen had a considerable part to play in the lives of children.

As in Chimbu, there were recognised ways for a husband to help his wife in Port Moresby, but there was little opportun-ity for a wife, unless she was earning money, to help her hus-band. A husband might help his wife with the cooking or wash-ing the dishes, but he would never help her by washing clothes. It is these activities which a husband is prepared to assist with that are most likely to become joint activities in fam-ilies where a joint conjugal relationship is developing; this was already the case with one family in Port Moresby that appeared to be developing a comparatively joint conjugal role-relationship, although the basis for this might not be a de-sire for a companionate type of relationship.

Social category II families

These families lived in better houses and had slightly better-paid jobs than families in social category I, although income was not the most important factor in determining life-style. Husbands, and some of the wives, had more social re-lationships with non-Chimbu than did those in category I, less contact with kin, and households were smaller, so that the families were more individuated. Perhaps as a concomitant of this, some families emphasised the care and guidance of their children more than did the category I parents. In general, their conjugal relationships and social networks were very similar to those of the category I families and very distinct from the family relationships of category III families.

Social category III families

These families were very distinct from the other families in terms of the husband-wife relationship and their social networks. The husbands had a very wide, loose-knit network of social relationships, both formal and informal, with non-Chimbu people of all races. In addition, husbands and wives had a close social network of friends comprised of non-Chimbu, Chimbu and the kin with whom they chose to have close relation-ships.

Many social activities were performed as a family, and many of their friends visited them as a family. They were concern-ed and ambitious for their children to have a Western-type

life in the future. The husbands had travelled abroad and had
a fair knowledge of Western-type family life. They encouraged
their children in educational activities when they were at
home, and their wives supported them to the best of their abil-
ity.

These wives were not bored at home.[1] They were busy looking after their children and sewing to make a little money.
They joined in conversations with their husband's visitors,
and many of these visitors brought their wives with them. At
the same time these wives continued to maintain strong ties
with their own kinsmen and when their husbands were away on
long trips overseas they usually went back to their home
areas, but not necessarily to their parents' home because they
insisted on living where the children could go to a primary
'A' school. One wife stayed in Port Moresby for several months
while her husband was away, but found life boring; with no
transport of her own she became tired of being in the house so
much and became tense because of the responsibility of having
to cope with domestic problems, such as sick children, on her
own.[2]

The conjugal role-relationship of the category III families
was much less segregated than that of the category I and II
families, and the wives would probably have liked it to be
even less segregated. The husbands had considerable demands
made on their time through work, political interests, or community activities, so it might be difficult for them to practise a more joint relationship. In any case they retained
more segregated, more traditional views about marriage than
did their wives, but because of their commitment to the Western ideology of life in general they would not be willing to
practise some aspects of traditional life which in fact they
favoured.

In these couples tension seemed to occur in the husbands
rather than the wives. The husbands had to contend with con-
flicts of attitudes, with the fast pace of life, responsible
jobs, and a feeling of insecurity, especially economic insecurity in terms of their aspirations. This latter was
clearly demonstrated by the very great delight shown by one
of the husbands and his wife when, as a result of the marriage
of a relative to a non-Chimbu, he was given a piece of land
in the highlands to develop as a pig farm with his affinal
relative.

---

[1] One was working full time.

[2] Kinsman friends of hers or her husband's would assist her
if any major problem arose.

Links between urban and
rural Chimbu

Only 3 of the 20 families did not state that they planned eventually to settle down in Chimbu or a neighbouring area. Many wanted to go in the near future, but for varying reasons this did not seem likely. Of the 3 exceptions, 2 were non-committal about settling back in Chimbu but certainly intended to visit from time to time. The other family, the husband coming originally from the Gulf District[1] and whose two eldest children were being looked after by the husband's sister, were doubtful whether for financial reasons, they would ever be able to go to Chimbu even for a visit, although the wife would certainly have liked to.

Most social category I wives would have returned to Chimbu immediately if given the opportunity, as they were not happy in Port Moresby. The exception was wife M whose husband had a well-paid job. She had been to Chimbu recently on holiday and found it very dirty, due, she said, to a shortage of water near the house. Wife K, who was earning so much, also did not wish to return for the time being.

Husbands were not so keen to return immediately, except for a visit, because they had worked out a more satisfying way of life in the city than had their wives, and possibly because there were few younger men living in some parts of Chimbu. Although many wives were not happy in Port Moresby, the number of married as well as single women coming to the city increased during 1972. Some of these returned, disillusioned, after a few months, sometimes, with the connivance of their husbands, earning their fare back from the proceeds of short-term prostitution.

Links with kinsmen in the Chimbu were maintained through letters and news brought by the continual flow of people to and from Chimbu. When these people came to Port Moresby they were given hospitality and assistance by their kinsmen already in the city, and when these kinsmen went back to Chimbu, to visit or to stay, they were given assistance by kinsmen there. In contrast, when category III families went to Chimbu they were expected to give assistance to their kinsmen. Many unsophisticated relatives in rural Chimbu looked upon their young, educated kinsmen from the city with great respect and awe and one husband found this very embarrassing. Two of the

---

[1] Consequently they had no land in Chimbu.

[2] Kinsmen who have not been to Port Moresby will expect presents from kinsmen returning from the city.

category III families intended to return to Chimbu eventually,
the third couple simply saying that they would go 'wherever
God sent them'.

Why did so many of the families wish to return to Chimbu?
Emotional ties with their kin? Perhaps. Emotional ties to
the land and a desire to die near the home of their ancestor
spirits? Perhaps, but few of the families seemed close to
death and none of them expressed this wish. Probably the most
important reason was a desire to work for oneself rather than
for an employer. In Chimbu a man who works hard can see the
results for himself in prestige and perhaps more wives; but in
Port Moresby none of the husbands considered that they were
being well paid for what they did, nor gained adequate prestige from their work. Nearly all hoped to amass some capital
and start a business of their own in Chimbu, but at the same
time were realistic enough to recognise that this dream might
never eventuate. Some had given up hoping, like one couple
who did not say that they were planning to return to Chimbu
but simply that they would follow their son wherever he wanted
to go. They were pinning their hopes for the future on their
son (three years old at the time of my study).

The desire for the company of relatives still in the Chimbu,
for the sight of tree-clad mountains and highlands scenery and
their own land kept alive the wish to return, eventually, to
Chimbu; all families disliked the heat of the coast. No-one
expressed any dislike of living among alien groups. Added to
this, for the category I families, was nostalgia and the desire to live according to the way they had been brought up.[1]
Although people do not realise that the old ways may be incompatible with education, businesses and Christianity, all
of which they desire in the midst of the barren, restrictive
life of Port Moresby, it is the life, however unrealistic,
which they look forward to in the future. But for the present
the pragmatic Chimbu in Port Moresby is interested in trying
to accumulate money.

Conclusion

This study neither proves nor disproves Bott's hypothesis
that the degree of segregation in the role-relationship of
husband and wife varies directly with the connectedness of
the family's social network. Chimbu and Londoners' conjugal

---

[1] Including involvement in gift exchanges, singsing and
'turning head' ceremonies as well as the consumption of local
vegetables.

role practices and attitudes were so different that it was
impossible to compare them on the basis of the concepts used
by Bott. The social network patterns of Chimbu and London
families were also very different. Actual kin, and people
who in the city are considered as kin, feature prominently in
the social networks of Chimbu, making considerable demands
upon as well as contributions to, husbands and wives. It seems
that the more ties there are with kin the fewer ties there are
between husband and wife, and that a change in one set of relationships will have repercussions on the other. In support
of this it seems that category III families in this study had
a tendency to more joint conjugal behaviour, and to a lesser
extent, in their attitudes towards the conjugal relationship
than did social category I families, although there were exceptions. They were more selective in their relationships
with kin, and had a smaller proportion of kin in their networks than did families in the other two social categories.
However, whether variations in the degree of connectedness
was also a significant factor in the networks of the different families cannot be stated because of the lack of adequate
data and the differences in the social networks of Chimbu and
London families. Certainly the networks of category I families were more closely knit and more segregated than those of
category III families, the latter having two distinct sections
in their networks, a loose-knit section of formal relationships
and a close-knit section of kin and friends. Bott's families
did not have networks organised in this way.

The study has practical implications for the understanding
of the problems of social development in Papua New Guinea. It
shows that a changed physical and economic environment has
forced some changes in practices, while attitudes, even among
social category III families, may have remained traditional.
This situation is likely to cause tension in individuals; some
people, especially those in social categories I and II, have
had no opportunity to learn new attitudes or ways of socialising their children. In the context of internal and external
family relationships, this study shows, both theoretically and
practically, some of the ways that Chimbu families have attempted to come to terms with the urban environment of Port Moresby.

Appendix A

Interview guide[1]

A[2]

1. Family.   Husband / Wife   responses
2. Name(s).
3. Occupation(s).
4. Education.
5. Religion.
   If Christian - church member/baptised/other.
6. Tribe/language group.
7. Where born.
8. Languages spoken well.
9. Languages spoken at home.

Topic I. Port Moresby residence

1. Where living.
2. How long has he/she been living in Port Moresby?
3. Other places outside the tribal area where he/she has lived,
   and for how long?
4. Type of house now living in.
5. Composition of present household. Comments, i.e., how permanent.
6. Is there a garden? What is in it? If not, why not and would
   he/she like to have one?
7. Do they intend to spend the rest of their lives in Port
   Moresby? Why?
8. Why do they live where they do?
9. How often does he/she return to their tribal area?

B

1. Husband/wife.   Family
2. Name(s).
3. Appearance.
4. Fluency in English, Pidgin, and whether communications were
   a problem at the interview.
5. Comments on husband/wife dependency.

Topic I. Port Moresby residence

1. Comments on neighbourhood and accessibility.
2. Comments on house structure, etc.
3. Comments on house - interior - cleanliness, contents, degree
   of overcrowding, etc.

---

[1] A number of questions included in this guide are not directly relevant to the
study of conjugal relationships or social networks, but were asked in connection
with work being carried out for the Department of Public Health in Papua New Guinea.

[2] Section A contains direct questions and section B covers my comments on people's
attitudes and my direct observations. See p.8 for further details.

147

4. Comments on garden.
5. Comments on plans for the future.
6. What do they think about life in Port Moresby?

<u>A</u>

1. Husband/wife.   Family
2. Name(s).

Topic II. Marital and family status

1. How many wives does he/her husband:
   a) have now?   Where are they?
   b) has had?   What has happened to them?
2. In what position is the present wife being interviewed?
3. By what method were they married, and why? Was this what
   he/she wanted?
4. Were/are his/her parents happy about it?
5. How did they come to marry <u>each</u> other?
6. What is a good husband?
7. What is a good wife?
8. Why do people get married?
9. How long have they been married?
10. How many children does he/she have here in Port Moresby?
11. How many children would he/she like to have altogether/by
    this wife/your self? Who decides this, and why? By what
    means can they limit family size?
12. Why do/don't some men bring their wives to Port Moresby?
    Comments.
13. In Chimbu wives live in their own houses, and men live in
    men's houses. What happens in town, and which arrangements
    does he/she like best?
14. What relatives does he/she have in Port Moresby?
    Name.   Sex.   Relationship.   Occupation.   Residence.

<u>B</u>

1. Husband/wife.   Family
2. Name.

Topic II. Marital and family status

1. General attitude to marriage; to own marriage.
2. Attitude to polygyny.
3. Does his/her marriage seem secure?
   Comments.
4. Which do they think is better, married life in Port Moresby
   or in Chimbu? Are they happy with their house, etc?
5. Is their attitude to family size realistic, and does religion
   come into their attitude?

<u>A</u>

1. Name.   Family
2. Wife present. Yes/No.

Topic III. Husband's activities and attitudes

1. Occupation.
2. Hours of work.
3. How does he travel to and from work and how long does
   it take?

4. How long has he had the job?
5. What is the pay?
6. How does he spend it?
7. What things would he like to have?
8. How does he usually spend:
   a) his evenings?
   b) his weekends?
9. Does he play sport? If so, what and how often? Would he like to play?

10.	Does he gamble?	Regularly.
		Sometimes.
	Who with?	Relationship.
11.	Does he drink?	Regularly.
		Sometimes.
	Who with?	Relationship.
12.	Does he chew betel nut -	No?
		Sometimes?
		Regularly?

13. What else does he do in his free time?
14. Whom does he visit regularly?
    a) With his wife:
    Name.   Sex.   Relationship.   Tribe.
    b) Without his wife.
15. What things do he and his wife do together?
16. Does he help his wife? How? Is this customary?
17. Does his wife help him? How? Is this customary?
18. How many children does he have? (biological and adopted)
19. Whose are they? (i.e., do they belong to their father, their mother or to both parents?) Who is in charge of them?
20. How many children would he like to have? Who regulates this?
21. Does anyone else put money into, or give presents to, the household?
22. Day's activities.
23. What does his wife do if she runs out of food and money?
24. What does he do?
25. Day's budget.

B

1. Name.   Family
2. Wife present. Yes/No.

Topic III. Husband's activities and attitudes

1. What does he think about Port Moresby life? How does it compare with tribal life? What are its problems, frustrations, etc?
2. Where does he get his companionship and emotional satisfaction?
3. In the Chimbu, men's work and women's work are kept separate. What happens in Port Moresby? Are men's and women's work and responsibilities the same in Port Moresby or in what way does he see them as different to in the Chimbu? How much does he know about traditional customs?
4. How adjusted to town life is he?
5. How does living in the same house with his wife affect their sexual relationship?
6. Does he think that witchcraft and sorcery exist in Port Moresby? Who is involved?
7. What part does religion play in his life?
8. Does he seem very dependant upon people other than his wife? Comments.

150

<u>A</u>.

1. Name. Family
2. Husband present. Yes/No.

Topic IV. Wife's activities and attitudes

1. a) Is she working for money?
       What kind of work?
       What hours?
       How much does she earn, and how is the money spent?
       What arrangements, if any, are made for the children?

    b) Has she ever worked (i) before marriage?
                           (ii) since marriage and living in Port Moresby?
2. Does she know how much her husband earns?
3. Who decides how the money will be spent, and what are the arrangements?
4. Is she satisfied with the financial arrangements?
5. Does anyone besides her husband give her money?
    Explain.
6. What does she do if she runs out of food and money?
7. What things would she like to buy?
8. What does she usually do each day?
9. What does she usually do at the weekends?
10. What are her duties to the family?
11. What are her husband's duties to the family? Does he do them?
12. Whom does she visit regularly?
    Name.   Sex.   Relationship.   Tribe.
    a) with her husband.
    b) without her husband and with whom?
13. What kind of things do she and her husband do together?
14. Does her husband help her? How? Is this customary?
15. How many children does she have and how many by her present husband?
16. Of the children who are in Port Moresby, do they belong to their
    father, their mother, or to both their parents?
    Who is in charge of them?
17. How many children would you like to have? Who regulates this?
18. Do you chew betel nut - No?
                           Sometimes?
                           Regularly?
19. Does she drink alcoholic drinks - No?
                                      Sometimes?
                                      Regularly?
20. Day's diary and budget. Presents given and received.

<u>B</u>.

1. Name. Family
2. Husband present. Yes/No.

Topic IV. Wife's activities and attitudes

1. What does she think about life in Port Moresby? How does it
    compare with tribal life? What are its problems, frustrations, etc?
2. Where does she get her companionship and emotional satisfaction?
3. In Chimbu men's work and women's work are kept separate. What
    happens in Port Moresby? Are men's and women's work and respon-
    sibilities the same in Port Moresby, or do they differ in the
    Chimbu? How much does she know about traditional customs?
4. How adjusted to town life is she?
5. How does living in the same house with her husband affect their
    sexual relationship? What is her attitude to family size?

6. Does she think witchcraft and sorcery exist in Port
   Moresby? If so, who is involved?
7. What part does religion play in her life?
8. Does she seem very dependant upon people other than
   her husband? If so, who?

<u>A</u>.

1. Name(s).   Family
2. Husband/wife/both.

Topic V. Social relationships

What transport do they normally use? a) The husband?

b) The wife?

Informal relationships

1. People who have visited them during the past week.

   <u>Name</u>   <u>Sex</u>   <u>Relationship</u>   <u>Occupation</u>   <u>Tribe</u>   <u>Transport</u>   <u>Length of visit</u>

2. People who he/she/they visited during the past week.

   <u>Name</u>   <u>Sex</u>   <u>Relationship</u>   <u>Occupation</u>   <u>Tribe</u>   <u>Transport</u>   <u>Length of visit</u>

3. People he/she/they met casually and had conversation with, during
   the past week.

   <u>Name</u>   <u>Sex</u>   <u>Relationship</u>   <u>Occupation</u>   <u>Tribe</u>   <u>Transport</u>   <u>Length of visit</u>

Formal relationships

a) During the past week, b) does he/she/they regularly attend:-
   Church .
   Church meeting.
   School meeting.

   Sports. a) To play. b) To watch. c) A committee
            d) To train or umpire.

   Clinic or hospital   a) For treatment. b) Routine visit.
                          c) To visit a patient.

   A sorcerer.
   Women's club.
   A meeting of Chimbus. What kind?
   A meeting associated with work.
   A formal reception.
   Any other formal group or gathering of people.

Appendix B

Husband-wife division of labour[1]

Chimbu traditional society
Husband's duties:
Domestic sphere

a) Food production:

   i) Heavy gardening work, i.e.
fence making, chopping down
trees, burning off grass,
etc. Often done in association with subclan group.

  ii) Protect rights in land, i.e.,
claiming compensation for
damage, fighting invaders to
retain own land, in association with kin group.

 iii) Help to gather and chop firewood.

b) Home provision:

    Build the men's house and a
house for his wife in association with his kin group.

c) Children:

   i) Procreate children and insert
in the womb of his wife.

  ii) Socialise male children.

d) Health:

    Look after the health of him-
self and his family and kin
group by observing various
rules of behaviour.

Group sphere

a) Help kin group members in those
domestic spheres mentioned above
that may be carried out in association with other kin.

London society
Husband's duties:
Domestic sphere

a) Food production:

   i) Earns money through employment
or investment, etc , for the
purchase of food. Usually
purchasing is done by the wife.

  ii) May provide money from time to
time to pay a solicitor to
guard family's rights in property, etc.

 iii) Provide money to pay fuel bills
and buy stoves, etc

b) Home provision:

    Provide money to buy and furnish
a house for himself, his wife
and their children to live in.

c) Children:

   i) Contribute to the procreation of
children if they are desired.

  ii) Help with the socialisation of
children in association with
wife and school.

d) Health:

    Provide money for medical and
hospital treatment if and when
it is needed.

Group sphere

a) Help his close kin with money if
they are in great need.

---

[1] The more important activities only are considered.

152

b) Participate in dispute settlement activities if he is old enough.

c) Take part in ritual and gift-exchange activities with his kin group.

d) Keep in touch with his sisters and mother, and look after their interests if required.

e) Be hospitable to his wife's kin group members.

b) Serve on the jury or go to war if required.

c) Keep in touch with his mother (and other close kin if he wishes) through visits and/or letters and/or telephone calls.

d) Pay taxes to the politico-legal system and the education system.

Wife's duties:
Domestic sphere

a) Food production:

  i)   Plant, tend, weed and harvest most of the food crops.

  ii) Cook most of the vegetable foods.

  iii) Collect water and firewood.

b) Clothes:

  Make string for the making of pubic aprons, scarves and string bags.

c) The home:

  She may help her husband and his kin group with some of the lighter jobs in house building.

d) Children:

  i)   Look after children from conception.

  ii) Play an important part in socialising her daughters.

  iii) Look after her own and her husband's pigs.

Group sphere

a) Provide food for her husband's gift-exchanges.

b) Cook food for her husband's kin when they visit.

c) Keep in touch with her own natal group through visits.

Wife's duties:
Domestic sphere

a) Food production:

  i)   Purchase most of the food with money provided by her husband.

  ii) Do most of the cooking.

b) Clothes:

  May make some clothes, but mostly they are bought with money. Responsible for the washing and ironing of clothes.

c) The home:

  i)   If she goes out to work she may provide some money towards the house.

  ii) Keep the house clean inside.

d) Children:

  Has the main responsibility for looking after the young children, and plays an important part in caring for and socialising older children.

Group sphere

May spend a lot of time with her mother or sisters, or in formal groups such as clubs or societies.

Appendix C

Case histories

Social category I families

Family A

Education level: Husband: none; wife: none.

Residence: a) Place: Initially in house in the grounds of the institution where the husband was working. Later they moved to a new house in a low-
cost housing suburb.

            b) Type of house: The first one was a wooden-frame house on
stilts, with two bedrooms, a lounge-kitchen, and a shower room; a pan toilet outside; power. The second house had three small bedrooms (the dividing walls did
not reach to the ceiling), a small lounge-kitchen, and a shower room; a pan toilet
outside; power. In the first house a wood stove was provided, and basic furniture.
In the second house there was no furniture or stove, only a kerosene burner.

Husband's work: Chief cook.

Wife's work: Occasional domestic employment, but most of the time she
was not working. She did not speak Pidgin.

Type of marriage: a) Method of marriage: Traditional, by arrangement and with
brideprice, but the wife was very keen to marry this man.

            b) Present conjugal relationship: Highly segregated.

Length of stay in   Husband: 3½ years (he had been in Port Moresby for nearly
 Port Moresby: 2 years during 1961-62); wife: 3 years.

Notes: This husband had two wives, one in Chimbu and one in Port Moresby. Although
they considered the education of their children to be very important, this couple
was very traditionally minded. They held a funeral feast in Port Moresby when the
husband's mother died in Chimbu; when the wife was ill they killed a chicken and
cooked food in the traditional style, which she and her husband and relatives ate;
after quarrelling with her husband the wife gave him a chicken. The husband led
his life and the wife hers. When they moved to the low-cost housing suburb their
house was always crowded with both the husband's and the wife's relatives who
stayed there indefinitely. At the institution house, relatives and others were
not allowed to stay without official permission.

After the husband returned from leave he left his first wife (A) in the
Chimbu, because she was not well, and brought his second wife and another son
back with the four children who had been in Port Moresby before. Three married
couples and their children looked after his house while he was away and in spite
of polite suggestions, they would not move out on the family's return. The son
who had just arrived in Port Moresby found the overcrowded house intolerable,
and slept at the homes of various other relatives.

This couple brought their children up according to the concepts and rules
of traditional behaviour, not being aware that such socialisation might not be
the most suitable for the type of social situation in which the children were
living.

Family B

Education level: Husband: none; wife: none.

Residence: a) Place: In a small shanty settlement on the top of a ridge.
All the houses in the settlement were built of scrap timber and corrugated iron
pieces. There were a few small garden plots, but the ground was stony, and very
dry during the dry season. During my study some new houses were put up, reducing
the amount of ground available for vegetable gardens. Different parts of the
settlement were inhabited by people from different parts of Papua New Guinea, with
no communication between the people of these different sections. The Chimbu
section contained people from different parts of Chimbu, but although they used
the same footpaths (which was not the case with the people from the different
sections), there was no socialising between them. There was no power, no drainage and no water (except off the iron roofs during the wet season). People got
their water, with or without permission, from the high-covenant homes below the
ridge. Schools and shops were only a few minutes' walk away. Most of the residents were men, either single or married men without their wives. When I first
visited the Chimbu section, six women lived there: five arrived during the study,
and one woman came and left.

                     b) Type of house: One-room wooden shack with a leaking corru-
gated iron roof; one wooden bed (home-made) and one chair; no windows.

Husband's work: Domestic servant.

Wife's work: Domestic servant.

Type of marriage: a) Method of marriage: Elopement. No brideprice was paid.
A kinsman of the husband took a photograph of the husband to Chimbu, and the wife,
who was married to an older man then in gaol, saw the photo and decided she liked
the man. When the husband went on leave, the wife met the man through her brother
and they eloped. At this time the husband was married to another woman. This
woman still considered herself married to the husband, but the husband was not
sure about it. He had custody of their child, who was in Port Moresby with him
and his new 'wife'.

                     b) Present conjugal relationship: Fairly independent. The
husband lived in Port Moresby for over three years without a wife, and had many
kinsmen then, including fourteen living at the same shanty settlement, during the
period of my study. He hardly changed his drinking habits since his wife arrived.
He, taught her to do domestic work, and her money, which she controlled, was used
to buy food and clothes and cigarettes. She had no kinswomen nearby, and some of
her few kinsmen in Port Moresby were angry because she ran off with another man,
who did not pay brideprice. She was lonely and dependent on her husband for
emotional and sexual satisfaction.

Length of stay in   Husband: 4½ years; wife: ½ year.
  Port Moresby:

Notes: Some people considered this couple to be married, others did not. The 2½-
year-old son from the husband's first marriage was something of a problem, as he
would not obey either the husband or his new wife. He spent much time with the
husband's kinsmen. Before coming to Port Moresby the child would hardly have
known his father, nor his new mother. By European standards this would be considered to be emotionally damaging for the child, but I am unable to say whether
this would be so for Chimbu children who may have spent much time with various
kinsfolk rather than being brought up solely by their mother and father. One
adopted child (family J) was said to be almost unmanageable, and another (family
N) was said to be difficult to manage. One biological child was said to be
difficult for his mother to handle, but his father said that he had no difficulty
with him (family A).

       In 1973 this couple, together with some of the husband's kinsmen, moved to
another shanty settlement.

Family C

Education level: Husband: none; wife: none.

Residence: a) Place: In the same section of the shanty town in which couple B lived, but in a compound household of people from a different part of Chimbu.

b) Type of house: The house was built of scrap timber and corrugated iron pieces. There was no power, water or drainage. The house consisted of four units. Two single men lived in one room at the end, and did not form part of the compound household centred on three married couples who cooked and ate together but did not pool their money. The sleeping arrangements for the members of this compound household were as follows:

Room 1: Family C and their child.
Room 2: A kinsman and a man from the same village as the husband C.
Room 3: A family comprised of a man, his wife and daughter (not included in my study). A cousin of the husband and a traditional trading partner.
Room 4: Family E and their three children.
Room 5: The brother of husband C. Halfway through the study they were joined by a married couple and their baby, who had been evicted from their accommodation because of a fight. Both the husband and wife were related to family C and to the couple in room 3.

Husband's work: Labourer.

Wife's work: None, except watching her child.[1] She was pregnant. Sometimes she cooked but usually other members of the compound household cooked for her. Sometimes she went shopping. In the compound household the wives often cooked at the same time over the same fire, and sometimes they used the same pans, but when they had money they bought their food separately, although it was served communally. Those with no money to buy food still got a share if they were present when the food was served.

Type of marriage: a) Method of marriage: Arranged by kinsmen of both parties. Traditional, with brideprice being collected and paid by his agnates. The marriage was blessed in the church. Husband was already working in Port Moresby, and he returned to the city soon after his marriage, leaving the wife with her parents. He sent her fare to come to Port Moresby about three years later.

b) Present conjugal relationship: Highly segregated. The husband was very tired after work, and simply ate and slept. At weekends he drank at a hotel, although sometimes when others played cards at the settlement, he and his wife watched or played. He seemed to get emotional satisfaction from his drinking companions, she from the other women of the compound household and from her child.

Length of stay in   Husband: about ten years; wife: she was first here for two
Port Moresby: years and returned home; she had been back for another two
years.

Notes: This husband established a pattern of heavy drinking when he was in Port Moresby on his own, and he continued to drink heavily, mainly with a Kerema workmate. Often the wife had no money to buy food and had to depend on the other families in the compound household for food. However, sometimes only three of the men living in the household had paid employment. All adults in this household were avid gamblers.

In 1973 this family returned to Chimbu, using the wife's earnings to pay the fare. It was suggested that later they may have left Chimbu and gone to Lae.

---

[1] Later (1972) this woman found domestic work nearby, and some of the other women in the settlement looked after her children, including bottle-feeding the new baby, while she was working.

Family D

Education level: Husband: none; wife: none.

Residence: a) Place: At the same shanty settlement as families B and C.
They belonged to the same dialect group as family C.   Later they moved out to a
settlement fourteen miles from Port Moresby where the wife's cousin had a small
pig and poultry farm (see family F).   They also leased a block of land in a new
suburban settlement zone where they planned to build their own home.   In 1973
they moved into the urban resettlement[1] zone so that the eldest child could go to
school.   Their house in this settlement was provided by the husband's employer.

b) Type of house: A two-room shack, without power, water or
drainage.   It was built by one of the wife's relatives, who with his wife were
the first people to live on this ridge.

Husband's work: Labourer

Wife's work: Looking after the children.   Sometimes she collected disused
soft drink bottles to earn a little money.

Type of marriage: a) Method of marriage: The wife said that she was a young
girl when her father, and a relative of her present husband who had married into
her kin group, more or less forced her to marry her present husband, whom she did
not know, and who was a lot older than she.   They tried to persuade her by saying
that the man was wealthy, which turned out not to be true.   She was tricked into
going to Port Moresby, and once there, could not run away as there were no Sinasina women there at that time.   Once she had children she felt that she couldn't
leave her husband, and found that he was good natured even if he never had any
money.   Then a brother-in-law persuaded the couple to get baptised and to be
married in church.   They had three small children at the time of my study and the
wife was pregnant again.   The wife's cousin thought very badly of them for having
children in such quick succession.

b) Present conjugal relationship: Segregated.   The husband
worked long hours for low wages.   They frequently played cards and gambled.   The
husband also drank.   The wife spent much time with the women at the compound house
during the day, and they were a source of emotional satisfaction, as were her two
children.   The son had to be handled by his father, and sometimes accompanied him
to work.

Length of stay in   Husband: 17 years; wife: 5 years.
Port Moresby:

Notes: The wife wanted to go back to Chimbu because she was always short of money
and food and had no work to do in Port Moresby, but they had no money for the fares.
The husband did not want to go back because he was afraid that his children would
be harmed by witchcraft in Chimbu.   He said that there was no witchcraft in Port
Moresby.

Family E

Educational level: Husband: none; wife: none.

Residence: a) Place: In the compound household of family C i.e., in a
shanty settlement.

b) Type of house: As for family C.

Husband's work: Labourer

---

[1] In these resettlement zones married men can rent a block of land for $5 annually.
During the first two years they may live in any type of house, but after two years
they are expected to have built a house of permanent materials to certain minimum
standards.
    In these areas there are piped water stands to be used by 5 households, and
electric power will be available as the settlement becomes established.

Wife's work: None, apart from a little cooking and housework, and looking after the children.

Type of marriage: a) Method of marriage: Arranged by the respective parents, but once the girl saw the good coffee gardens that her husband's people had, she was keen to marry him. Soon after they married the husband went away to work on a plantation for eighteen months. He then returned to Chimbu for a short time, before going to work in Port Moresby. After about another eighteen months his wife bought her own plane ticket from coffee she sold, and came down to Port Moresby without telling her husband she was coming.

b) Present conjugal relationship: Segregated. The husband worked long hours, and drank heavily. Sometimes he and his wife drank together with other members of the compound household and visitors. They both played cards and gambled as part of a larger group of Sinasina people.

Length of stay in   Husband: 2½ years; wife: 1 year.
Port Moresby:

Notes: The wife was an independent type of woman who seemed to be able to look after herself in many respects. She gave birth to her third child (and third daughter) during my fieldwork. She did not like Port Moresby because there was no work for her to do. She was thinking of leaving the eldest child, who went to school, with her husband and going back to Chimbu if she could find money for the fares. There appeared to be no strong emotional tie between husband and wife and she believed that economically she would be better off in Chimbu. The husband did not want to go back to Chimbu to live because there were only old people there - and women. He said he would not waste money on prostitutes in Port Moresby, but work hard and save money, as he did in the past.

In 1973 they, with a family living in the same household but not included in my sample, moved in to a shanty house in an urban resettlement area. Later one family will move onto an adjoining block of land.

Family F

Education level: Husband: standard 3 at a mission school; wife: none.

Residence: a) Place: Servant's quarters of house where wife was working. Certain restrictions were applied by the owners: only first degree relatives could sleep there and then usually only for three months; parties could not be held and card playing was strictly forbidden.

b) Type of house: One-bedroomed fibro-walled house with shower and flush toilet, drainage and power; wood stove; no furniture.

Husband's work: Driver. But he also worked at weekends driving his own three-ton passenger truck. After work, several times a week he went out to the small farm of pigs and poultry which he owned fourteen miles from Port Moresby.

Wife's work: Domestic servant. She also drove their utility truck out to the farm, and fed the animals with her husband or other relatives. She also cooked for her family and did the usual domestic chores.

Type of marriage: a) Method of marriage: The husband was already married to a Papuan woman when he went to the Chimbu on leave, without his Papuan wife. There his relatives pointed out his present wife to him, saying that she was a hard worker with a pleasant disposition. They met one day, and her brother told her that this man was a good man with plenty of money. They decided to marry the next day. She went to stay with his mother and he returned to Port Moresby. About eighteen months later he sent the money for her brideprice and the fare to Port Moresby. She lived in the house with the Papuan wife, but the latter became crosser and crosser, and eventually left, taking her child with her. (Polygyny was never so widespread among coastal people as it was, and still is, in the highlands; there would be few Papuan coastal men who are polygynists today.) The husband now thinks that one wife was enough for any man (he and his wife were both studying to become Jehovah's Witnesses).

b) Present conjugal relationship: A joint economic partnership. Kin ties of both husband and wife were still very strong with first-degree relatives, but not for less close relatives. The couple welcomed restrictions on relatives coming to the house, and the husband refused to give money to people who were not working. He did however, give money regularly to the wife in family D who was his first cousin; her husband was working, but for low wages, and they had three children.

Length of stay in   Husband: 11 years; wife: 4 years.
Port Moresby:

Notes: The husband obtained the land for his farm from local tribesmen who adopted him soon after he arrived in Port Moresby as a boy (he came to provide company for an older brother).[1] Both husband and wife worked and saved very hard. The husband had no time for people who did not work regardless of the circumstances. When he and his wife go to Chimbu on leave he may leave her there and come back by himself while she establishes a coffee garden or runs a store. There seemed to be little emotional or sexual significance in the marriage relationship, and the husband sent for his brother to come down to Port Moresby to help him and to keep him company because he felt lonely. During fieldwork his sister and mother-in-law came to stay with them. Having severed ties with their kinsmen in general, they may have felt the need for more contact with their close relatives. This was the case when, after moving house twice, when the wife changed her employers she finally took a non-residential position and the family went to live with relatives. However, when the husband was gaoled for his part in a fight, it was his wife who bailed him out, in contrast to the more usual situation where a collection of agnatic kinsmen pay court fines for their kinsman.

Family G

Education level: Husband: No formal education but several years of mission education; wife: standard 3.

Residence: a) Place: A self-help low-cost housing settlement where it was hoped that families would build their own houses to a specified minimum standard, or better. There was no power or drainage in the house this family occupied. There were tap stands at regular intervals. Facilities and standards were better than in the shanty settlements, but not as good as in the low-cost housing suburbs.

b) Type of housing: This couple shared half of a two-bedroomed house with a large verandah but no sitting room, with two other Chimbu couples and a varying number of single men, all from the same area of Chimbu. The house was of wood, with an iron roof. This was a compound household, but the Chimbu kept separate from the Eastern Highlands people who lived in the other half. The house belonged to two expatriate single men, for the use of their respective domestic servants and wives, but the other people moved in with these two couples. The Chimbu wives, or their husbands, bought their food separately, but it was cooked at the same time, sometimes in the same, sometimes in different pots, and served together. The single men rarely contributed to the cost of the food, but if present when it was dished up, they were given a share similar to that of everyone else.

Husband's work: He usually worked as a domestic servant, but during most of my research his employer was away and he received no leave pay. He bought a motor-mower with money sent from Chimbu and made some money cutting grass, but the machine frequently broke down.

Wife's work: Housework

Type of marriage: a) Method of marriage: Traditional exchange. Both sets of

---

[1] As more and more Chimbu relatives of the husband and wife came to Port Moresby this farm was developing into a Chimbu settlement associated with the Koiari people.

parents were against the marriage at first, but later changed their minds. The couple were baptised in Port Moresby, and then married in a church.

b) Present conjugal relationship: Joint. This couple were trying hard to organise their life on Christian principles, as they understood them. The husband and wife agreed that the husband had always been a man to help his wife. The main problem was that they had no children of their own, their son having been adopted. The wife had an operation, but still had not become pregnant, and the husband was cross with her on this matter. He had lost interest in sexual relations, saying that if he were not a Christian he would divorce his wife and marry another woman. In spite of this, their overall relationship appeared to be relatively joint.

Length of stay in   Husband: 2½ years; wife: 2½ years.
Port Moresby:

Notes: No complaints were made about the behaviour of the adopted son (he was adopted as an infant, and I was told that he did not know he was adopted). However, he only arrived in Port Moresby, having completed his primary education, shortly after I met this couple. When his parents went out cutting grass he sat at home doing nothing, but later one of his friends managed to get a job for him. A number of the single young men were allowed to stay at the house because the husband, who was the leader of this compound household, said it was the Christian thing to do, and otherwise they might wander around town and get into trouble. He insisted they come home by 8 p.m. each evening. A few months after my study ended this couple moved to an outstation with the husband's previous employer, who had returned from leave.

Family H

Education level: Husband: No formal education but a few years of mission training; wife: none.

Residence: a) Place: The same self-help housing settlement and house that family G lived in.

b) Type of house: They formed part of the same household as couple G, husband H's employer being part-owner of the house in which they lived.

Husband's work: Domestic servant, but for several weeks during the time of my study the employer was away on leave, and the husband had no pay. He had a power lawn mower, but did not cut grass very often.

Wife's work: Housework

Type of marriage: a) Method of marriage: There was some doubt about whether this couple were in fact married. The wife told me that it was their custom for brideprice not to be paid until after the first baby was born, but her baby was several months old and the husband still had no intention of collecting brideprice. Shortly before I left Port Moresby the wife told me that she wanted to go back to her parents, and was free to do so, and take the child, because no brideprice had been paid (she had no money to pay the fare back to Kundiawa). However her relatives in Port Moresby did not seem disposed to give her money for the fare.

The husband's first wife left him, and when he was in Chimbu for a short time, he met his present wife and seduced her. She ran away with him to Port Moresby, against her parent's wishes.

b) Present conjugal relationship: Segregated. This husband had no interest in his wife and even after his employer had returned, he gave his wife no money. He spent it on drink or gambling, or gave it to relatives. But he loved playing with his young son.

Length of stay in   Husband: 10 years; wife: 2 years.
Port Moresby:

Notes: This couple were interesting in that a neighbouring Papuan women made friends with the wife at a time when there were no other married couples living in the house. This Papuan woman could speak very little Pidgin, but the two women gave each other presents of food sometimes. The friendship began when the wife was on the road waiting for her husband to come home, and some nights he never came. The other women in the compound household referred to this Papuan woman as wife H's friend.

A few months after the research ended the house was burnt down. Their Papuan neighbours took this couple in for a few weeks. However, in time they lost patience with the husband, who was working but still gave his wife no money or food. Nor did he give them anything in return for looking after the wife and child. Finally they asked them to leave. They moved in with some other Chimbu and the wife found part-time domestic work.

Family I

Education level: Husband: none; wife: none.

Residence: a) Place: As for couples G and H.

b) Type of house: As for couple G.

Husband's work: Labourer

Wife's work: A minimum of housework.

Type of marriage: a) Method of marriage: It seems that the wife saw the husband once, when she was a young girl (not old enough to be married) and decided then that she was the man she wanted to marry. Meantime the husband was in Port Moresby. When the girl was older and found that her parents were considering another boy for her to marry she ran away to the parents of her present husband and told them that she wanted to marry their son. She stayed with them for a few months, and they decided that she would make a good wife for their son. Brideprice was agreed to and paid. The husband's father brought the wife to Port Moresby (I am not sure whether the son knew that he was being married in absentia), and was still in the city at the time of my research.

b) Present conjugal relationship: Segregated, although the husband said that a husband should help his wife with the cooking. He beat his wife a number of times, which upset his father and the other members of the compound household. The wife, who seemed to be very fond of her husband, said they were not serious quarrels. The husband continued to drink heavily at weekends. The marriage had not been consummated: they claimed they had no suitable opportunity due to the crowded conditions in which they lived. This would not be considered unusual in Chimbu tradition.

Length of stay in   10 years; wife: 4 months.
Port Moresby:

Notes: Some of the other members of the compound household suggested that this husband's behaviour towards his wife might indicate that he was rejecting her, but they did not really think so. If he did reject her, his kin group would forfeit the brideprice they paid, as he would be rejecting the girl without just cause. At the end of research the couple moved into servants' quarters where they lived on their own, but he still fought her a number of times. She claimed that he was justified: once she had been slow to cook food for his father when he visited them (because her husband had been very late coming home with the food). The father, however, did not feel that the beating was justified.

Later the wife quarrelled with her employer over her pay, and the couple left and went to live with the wife's cousin, (O). When the husband lost his job they went to live at Fourteen-Mile. They had been encouraged by their employer to buy a block of land in a new suburban resettlement scheme, but the husband refused - probably through laziness, and because he realised that in his present situation he had no housing or food expenses.

Family J

Education level: Husband: none; wife: none.

Residence: a) Place: Initially in the servant's quarters of one of the expatriate staff of the institution where the husband worked. When family A moved out of their house in the institution grounds, this family moved into it.

b) Type of house: The original servant's house was a one-roomed wooden house with a wooden bed inside. There was a sheltered cooking and laundry area outside, and a pan toilet. The house had power and piped cold water.

Husband's work: Cook.

Wife's work: Domestic servant and housework.

Type of marriage: a) Method of marriage: Traditional exchange that was instigated by the respective kin groups.

b) Present conjugal relationship: Joint.[1] The husband felt a responsibility to look after his wife in Port Moresby. As she worked for money and had a strong character he helped her with domestic chores on his own initiative. This may be related to the fact that they were both growing old and had no children, as well as to the urban situation, and the fact that the wife had a strong character.

Length of stay in   Husband: 3 years (he also spent 2 years in Port Moresby some
Port Moresby: years ago); wife: 2 years.

Notes: This husband was a polygynist but wife J was his first wife, the other wives having been divorced. He had no children by any of his wives, which may be the reason he had so many wives and why in Chimbu he felt free to have affairs with women and girls (i.e., he had no children who would be harmed, according to traditional belief, as a result of his sexual contact with women).

They had an adopted daughter (about seven years old) who both parents and other Chimbu described as a problem child in that she would not do what she was told. The husband said that this was because her mother, one of his ex-wives, was obstinate (children were said to take after their mother because she looked after them, it being believed that the mother had no direct biological connection with her children). He said he took little interest in the child other than feeding her because she was difficult, but perhaps her behaviour was a desperate attempt to gain some attention. The father was not worried because the girl was not going to school, and hinted that in a few years she would earn money as a prostitute.

Early in 1973 this husband and wife had a serious quarrel because a previous wife of the husband came to him for protection, claiming that her brother, who paid her fare to Port Moresby, was putting her on the streets as a prostitute. Husband J accepted this wife back, so wife J returned to Chimbu, taking the child with her.

Shortly after this the husband, who had been turned out of his previous accommodation, was allocated a Housing Commission house in an urban resettlement area. The family with whom he had been staying when he was without a house, moved in with him. In the meantime the brother of the returned fifth wife took her away, saying that husband J had no rights to her as he had not paid the fare to Port Moresby and that the brideprice he had paid earlier had been returned; the wife was sent to live with another man.

Family K

Education level: Husband: none, except as a catechist; wife: none.

Residence: a) Place: A shanty settlement in a valley on the outskirts of Port Moresby. All the inhabitants of this settlement came from the same area of

---

[1] This was not the case when they lived in Chimbu.

Chimbu, most of them being single men, or men whose wives were in Chimbu. Any Chimbu in Port Moresby from the Gumine sub-district who could find no other accommodation, came out here. Approximately half the men living here were un-employed. There was no power, water or drainage. Water was obtained from a tap about twenty minutes' walk away.

b) Type of house: A one-room shack made of bits of packing case and pieces of sheet iron. Cooking was done in the open. There was garden land on the hillside nearby.

Husband's work: Contact man for his wife.

Wife's work: Prostitute.

Type of marriage: a) Method of marriage: The wife was already married to another man, but she 'carried leg' with her present husband, they liked each other and went to live together. Her brother chased the husband away, but his kin group agreed to pay brideprice (they hesitated because she had never had any children).

b) Present conjugal relationship: This was very difficult to evaluate in terms of activities because there was so little in their lives. They were usually out all day and it was not possible for me to visit this settlement at night to observe activities that could be turned into talking points. Their economic activities were complementary, in Bott's terms, which she classified as segregated. Cooking consisted of boiling rice and opening a tin of fish or meat or a packet of mutton chops. Sometimes the wife did this, sometimes the husband, and sometimes his kinsmen, who were close neighbours. This Bott would classify as joint activity. Emotionally it was also difficult to judge. He seemed to have only an economic interest in his wife now that she had produced no children. She seemed both dependant upon him and attached to him, but it could be fear; her brother tried to make her give up prostitution and return to Chimbu, but she refused. She seemed to like both the work and the husband, but did not like the fact that he controlled all the money she earned for his own purposes.

Length of stay in   Husband: 11 years (with periods in Chimbu); wife: 1 year.
Port Moresby:

Notes: When I asked why they did not move into a better house in town now that they were earning so much money, the husband said that he had to live near his kinsmen for protection: some man might want to kill him and take his wife away. When they went out on business they were usually accompanied by a kinsman.

They were saving the money to buy another wife to give the husband children. The husband said that the wife did not like the idea, but had agreed to it. The wife, even when being interviewed alone, said that she did not mind. All she wanted was money.

The couple went home to Chimbu but were not made very welcome possibly because people did not approve of their behaviour or because they were not very generous with their earnings from it. On returning to Port Moresby they built a new house in the shanty settlement. They purchased a passenger-truck, hiring a Gumine man to drive it, and used this for the woman to go around on her business. Earnings had increased considerably since the research period.

Family L

Education level: Husband: none; wife: standard 1.

Residence: a) Place: The same shanty settlement, but in a different section to families B,C,D and E.

b) Type of house: A one-room shack full of clothes. One chair and two home-made beds. No power, water or drainage.

Husband's work: Supervisory cook.

Wife's work: Housework.

Type of marriage: a) Method of marriage: The husband wanted to marry her, but she wanted to marry someone else, to which her parents would not agree. He gave many presents to her parents, and his kinsmen chased the man she liked away. Her parents said that he had lots of money and pigs, and so she agreed to marry him. She was his second wife, the husband becoming a polygynist. It was a traditional exchange marriage with brideprice being paid. The mission would not allow a church wedding as he already had one wife.

b) Present conjugal relationship: Segregated. The wife wanted her husband to marry another wife to keep him company in Port Moresby and bear him children while she stayed in Chimbu looking after their coffee. The husband controlled the money, although she looked after it before some was banked. He made money gambling and she looked after his takings until it was banked. He said that he couldn't leave his wife at home alone in Port Moresby, as some man might accost her. Sexual relations had ceased as they had a two-year-old child who pulled at the breast from time to time. The husband was not happy about this, but the wife used to attack him with a knife if he approached her; his brothers agreed with the wife that his sexual demands were unreasonable at that time: he had a child only two years old and he must wait, they said. The wife wanted him to have relations with other women, but he refused on the grounds that it was against the church, that he might get venereal disease, or their child might get sick. The wife did not want to become pregnant again. I referred them to a family planning clinic, but the visit was not, they told me, satisfactory.

Length of stay in   Husband: 3 years (but had been in Port Moresby before);
Port Moresby: wife: 2 years.

Notes: This man said he could not marry another wife because he had several younger brothers and his kin had to buy wives for them, and he too would be expected to contribute. The wife said that if she stayed in Chimbu she could sell a lot of coffee and buy another wife for him. During fieldwork one of the husband's brothers and a brother-in-law arrived in Port Moresby to live with them. The husband had paid their fares. He wanted them for companionship (he already had a married sister and another brother in the city). This husband came from a large family. When their child was smaller the wife worked and used her money to pay for her father to come and visit them. Ties with their respective natal groups were strong for both husband and wife.

Late in 1972 the wife went to live with one of her brothers, but the husband maintained that they were still married, it was just that his employers had not given him a house as they had promised, and his wife did not like it at the shanty settlement without power and water. However, the couple continue to quarrel regularly over the wife's refusal to have sexual intercourse.

Family M

Education level: Husband: Form 3 and on-the-job training; wife: none.

Residence: a) Place: Low-cost housing suburb.

b) Type of house: The same as the one that family O moved into. However, there were many more people in this house than the couple M and their two children. When I began my study there was another married couple and their baby and a younger brother of the husband all living in the house. Then the husband's sister and her husband arrived, and they too stayed with them, in this two-bedroomed house. This household more or less formed a compound household with the house next door but one, where the husband's cousin and her husband lived, together with one of husband M's brothers. When I first met husband M he had a large desk in the house where he sat to write articles and letters, but the house became too crowded and he had to take it out. At that time an opossum was kept in a cage in the kitchen. They had two cats and nine dogs.

Husband's work: Journalist.

Wife's work: Housework.

<u>Type of marriage:</u>   a) Method of marriage: The husband was sending presents to this wife when he was married to another woman whom he didn't like. He paid for this first wife himself, but apparently he did not know her and when they met he did not like her. He never brought her to Port Moresby. He then sent for his present wife, for whom he had not paid brideprice, and married her in church in Port Moresby. The first wife was living with the husband's parents and evidently considered herself to be married to him, although he considered that their marriage had ended. He had the child from his first marriage and gave it to his second wife, who now considered it to be her own.[1]

b) Present conjugal relationship: It is difficult to evaluate couple M's conjugal relationship in Bott's terms. The wife was the dominant partner. In such a household there was little opportunity for a close relationship. There were many other people about to help the wife with her domestic duties. The wife went visiting with her husband but people mostly came to visit the husband, who was heavily involved in both church and political affairs. The wife did not participate in these activities, apart from going to church with her husband. Their relationship was segregated, as much by circumstances as the attitude of the partners.

<u>Length of stay in</u>   Husband: 5 years; wife: 2 years.
<u>Port Moresby:</u>

<u>Notes:</u> I found this the most difficult family to work with, for two reasons. Firstly, the husband might have felt inadequate, and therefore on the defensive, because his comparatively high level of education contrasted with his unsophisticated style of living, because he had an uneducated wife, or because of his somewhat contradictory marital status in view of the fact he was a church councillor and worked hard for the mission. Secondly, there appeared to be some tension between husband and wife over the presence of one other married couple in the house. There was much gossip circulating among church members about wife M which I was unable to verify, but this couple may well have had things about which they preferred me not to know.

On returning from leave in the Chimbu the wife said she no longer wished to live in Chimbu - it was too dusty and dirty, with no piped water.

<u>Social category II families</u>

<u>Family N</u>

<u>Education level:</u>   Husband: standard 4, wife: standard 1.

<u>Residence:</u>   a) Place: In a residential compound belonging to the husband's employer. As a result of strictly enforced regulations by the employer life for the people living in the compound was different to that in other parts of Port Moresby. The same rules applied to families F and Q. As a result of these rules and patrols in the compound, women and young girls could walk in the compound area at night, and if their husbands were away they could stay alone and even sleep alone without fear.[2] This was not possible in other parts of Port Moresby. People varied in their attitudes towards these regulations. Most had mixed feelings: in some ways they wanted to be able to have relatives visit them freely and stay with them according to custom, but on the other hand, for economic reasons they were glad that there were some restrictions.

b) Type of house: Two-bedroomed fibro house with cement floor and iron roof. Power, running cold water, shower, flush toilet and drainage. Furniture was provided (two beds, four armchairs, table, upright chairs, cupboard).

---

[1] However, some time later this child was returned to its mother.

[2] There were also disadvantages in not having many people in a house, i.e., there was a greater possibility of intra-family abuses.

Husband's work: Mechanic

Wife's work: Housework only.[1]

Type of marriage: a) Method of marriage: Traditional exchange, initiated by the husband when he was in Chimbu on leave. He met his present wife when he visited a cousin. The wife went to stay with his mother who saw that the girl was a hard worker, and the husband's kinsmen paid the brideprice some months later (the husband had already returned to Port Moresby). Later they married in church.

                      b) Present conjugal relationship: Fairly segregated. Husband and wife seemed undecided whether the wife would return to Port Moresby after their next leave. The husband appeared disappointed that his wife had not yet borne him any children. He stressed many times that among Chimbu the husband was the 'boss', and his wife was very quiet and uncommunicative. However, when I asked her whether her husband was happy about the job I found for her (after I had completed my interviewing of them), she was most indignant at my question and replied angrily that it was up to her, and none of his business. At that time the husband did not know about the job (she had not told him when he came home for the weekend from a field patrol).

Length of stay in   Husband: 3½ years; wife: 2 years.
Port Moresby:

Notes: This couple adopted the wife's youngest sister, who was about eight years old and went to school. Both husband and wife said she was disobedient and wouldn't listen to them. She called them 'dad' and 'mum'. Whether her behaviour was related to the fact that she was adopted I cannot say, but it may be the result of the urban environment and going to school. In the Western education methods used in the schools children are taught to think for themselves rather than simply to do what they are told, and Chimbu parents may not be equipped to deal with children who have these new attitudes and approach to life. The children may not be guided by their parents to use their initiative in the right way, and parents may not give enough attention to their children in this new situation. In 1973 the wife found that this girl and her adoptive father were engaging in an illegal sexual relationship.

Family O

Education level: Husband: none; wife: none.

Residence: a) Place: Initially the wife and baby were living with family N, she being the clan sister of husband N. Her husband used to eat with them in the evenings, but due to the compound regulations he was not able to sleep there; he slept around with various Chimbu 'brothers'. Later they were allocated a one-bedroomed house in a low-cost housing suburb.

                      b) Type of house: A fibro house, on stilts, with an iron roof and wooden floor. Running cold water and power, but no drainage. Pan toilet. Kerosene burner, but no furniture provided with the house.

Husband's work: Carpenter.

Wife's work: Housework. She had a new baby.

Type of marriage   a) Method of marriage: Traditional exchange except that the husband paid the brideprice himself because he had no relatives in Chimbu. He was not a Chimbu but now considered himself to be one, and Chimbu accepted him as one of themselves. He went to Chimbu for employment purposes, and there met his wife.

                      b) Present conjugal relationship: Fairly joint. The wife seemed to be a strong character. Husband N was the only relative she had in Port Moresby and she said she did not want to become dependant upon him. She did not get on with her husband's relatives, who lived in a Port Moresby coastal village

---

[1] She did have domestic employment for a short time, but felt that she was not being adequately paid.

because, she said, only the younger ones spoke Pidgin, and they did not like her because when she stayed there for a few weeks she had malaria and did not help them.

Length of stay in   Husband: He came to Port Moresby as a boy with his father.
Port Moresby: About 1951 he started travelling and working throughout the country, returning to Port Moresby in 1967. During this time he spent four years in Chimbu and married in 1956.

                 Wife: 3 years. She travelled around to various government stations with her husband after they married.

Notes: Their two older children, both of whom were in high school in Port Moresby, had lived with the husband's sister for four to five years. When their parents obtained their own house, the younger came to stay with them for a short time, but the wife rarely if ever saw the older son. The husband's sister was angry with husband O when his wife unexpectedly, but after having some internal operation, became pregnant again. The wife worked as a domestic servant before she married, and had also worked in Port Moresby. When her employer found that she was pregnant she asked her to leave, and to vacate the servants' quarters. This was when she went to stay with her clan brother and his wife, family N. Husband O said he would never return to his village because there was too much sorcery there. Perhaps he felt nervous because he had refused to give money or help to some of his relatives.

During 1972-73 the husband was frequently out of work, or had to take labouring work. Both he and his wife tried very hard to find work. From time to time they had other Chimbu living with them, but not for more than a few months at a time. Either they were allocated accommodation i.e., army families, or they were asked to leave, by either the husband or wife, usually on the grounds that some aspects of their behaviour would be detrimental to their child. A domestic position was turned down for the same reason.

The wife established friendly relationships with the family next door, a Madang man married to a Buka woman. In mid-1973 a Kerema relative of the husband, a girl of about ten years, came to live with them to look after the child while wife O went out to work.

Family P

Education level: Husband: none, only on-the-job training; wife: none.

Residence: a) Place: Low-cost housing settlement, where they had lived for seven years.

                 b) Type of house: A wooden house on stilts, with a front verandah but no sitting room. Two bedrooms. A cooking space with a wood stove at the back of the house. Running cold water. Shower. Pan toilet. The wife kept apologising for the house, because, she said, it was old and no good. They did not want to move because there was a vacant lot next door which she had planted with vegetables.

Husband's work: Police constable.

Wife's work: Housework.

Type of marriage: a) Method of marriage: Traditional exchange followed by church blessing. She met him when he came to Chimbu on leave. Many girls wanted to marry him, but he wanted to marry his present wife. Her parents encouraged her, and his parents were also in favour.

                 b) Present conjugal relationship: Segregated. The wife became quite emotional when she talked about her brother who was transferred from Port Moresby two years ago; she obviously still missed him. They had no Chimbu neighbours but mixed with several from different parts of Papua New Guinea. The wife called one woman her 'age-mate' because she had no real age-mate in Port Moresby (in Chimbu custom there is a special, **very** close relationship between age-mates of the same sex). The husband drank heavily and gambled with men friends from various parts of the country.

Length of stay in   Husband: 8 years; wife: 7 years.
Port Moresby:

Notes: This couple seemed to be one of the best adjusted families from the point of view of urban living. But they were looking forward to returning to Chimbu when the husband retired in eighteen months. The husband was undecided whether his eldest daughter, who was in her last year in primary school, should go to high school. He finally decided to leave the choice to her, but his wife wanted the girl to continue with her studies.

Family Q

Education level: Husband: no formal education but several years of mission and on-the-job training. Had visited Australia three times for short-term training courses.

Wife: none.

Residence: a) Place: Employer's compound (see family N).

b) Type of house: see family N. The husband bought a refrigerator for his beer.

Husband's work: Security officer.

Wife's work: Housework.

Type of marriage: a) Method of marriage: The husband claimed that before he last went on leave his employers told him that he should come back married. When he was on leave a number of young girls wanted to marry him. He seduced his present wife and there was a court case. As the girl still wanted to marry him he agreed, in order to annoy her parents. Brideprice was paid but there was no church wedding, in spite of the protests of the priest at the mission station.

b) Present conjugal relationship: Segregated. This husband spent his free time drinking with workmates. He talked in a very derogatory fashion of women and married life. What drew him home was his daughter, of whom he was obviously very fond. The wife, who was about twenty years younger than her husband, appeared satisfied with his treatment, but spent her time with other Chimbu women living in the compound and her relatives who visited her.

Length of stay in   Husband: 9 years; wife: 3 years.
Port Moresby:

Notes: This family was classified as Category II because the husband's behaviour and attitudes were different in a number of ways of those of husbands in Category I. He took little interest in fellow Chimbu and associated mainly with workmates, both indigenous and expatriate. He claimed that these were the people who would help him in time of trouble, so they were the ones with whom he must be friendly. He claimed to prefer barbecues to mumu. He was ambitious for his children. On the other hand, his traditions were still part of him: his lack of companionship with his wife, his desire for sons, his threat to marry another wife if his wife had another daughter; pulling against some of these traditional attitudes was the force of the church which he still claimed was the one true religion (he used to be a catechist).

This family was on the borderline between Categories I and II because of the attitudes and behaviour of the wife, who had no interest in keeping her house clean or bettering herself and spent her time wandering from one Chimbu house to another. She was very dependant upon her husband and seemed well satisfied with him and his behaviour towards her and the children as he provided for her financially in spite of his heavy drinking, i.e., she was satisfied with a basically economic relationship with her husband.

Social category III families

Family R

Education level: Husband: standard 9 and tertiary training; wife: standard 6.

Residence: a) Place: High-covenant housing suburb.

                      b) Type of house: Two-bedroomed furnished duplex. Power,
piped hot and cold water. Electric stove. Flush toilet and drainage.

Husband's work: Clerk.

Wife's work: Housework and dressmaking.

Type of marriage: a) Method of marriage: A combined church and traditional
marriage. The husband and wife had corresponded but not met prior to the wedding.

                      b) Present conjugal relationship: Joint.[1] The husband helped
the wife in the home, and she helped him financially when she felt he needed
assistance. They had a car and spent much time visiting or entertaining joint
friends and relatives. However, the husband also had many business commitments
and political activities out of working hours.

Length of stay in   Husband: 4 years (and 1 year earlier before he was married);
Port Moresby: wife: 4 years.

Notes: The husband only lived a traditional Chimbu life until he was eight years
old. After that he was educated in boarding schools and worked in schools or towns.
The wife spent her childhood on mission stations in the Chimbu and in boarding
school. Their present social relationships were mainly with people who were school-
mates, workmates and educated relatives.

Occasionally the husband considered changing his employment, and did not seem
to be really settled in his work or satisfied that he was being given the chances
he deserved. When he was given some land by the husband of a cousin of his, who
married a man from a neighbouring part of the highlands where there was no land
shortage, he and his wife were overjoyed. They planned to start a pig farm in
conjunction with the cousin's husband. This man had rights to land in the Chimbu,
but for some years his brother had been using the land. The wife had no land.

Family S

Education level: Husband: form 4 (including two years at an Australian high
school), plus tertiary training; wife: form 3, plus tertiary training.

Residence: a) Place: In the grounds of the institution where the husband
was studying.

                      b) Type of house: Fibro, two-bedroomed house with power, run-
ning cold water and shower. Pan toilet. No restrictions on visitors or people
staying were mentioned, but no-one was staying on a regular basis; a young man
from the highlands ate with them every day because he was lonely where he was
living. There were chairs, a table, and two beds in the house.

Husband's work: Student.

Wife's work: Teacher.

Type of marriage: a) Method of marriage: Church wedding and no traditional wedding nor brideprice. The reason that no brideprice was given was because the husband was a student and because the Lutheran mission was against high brideprice.
Both the wife's parents were Lutherans. The couple had not planned to marry until
the husband had completed his studies, but when they went home on leave the parents
had arranged the wedding so they married.

---

[1] I use this term, as Bott does, in a relative sense. The conjugal role-relationship of this family was joint compared with that of most other families.

b) Present conjugal relationship: Joint. The husband had a lot of practical work to do in connection with his training, but his wife went with him when this was suitable and possible. She also felt she was helping her husband by entertaining his visitors. The husband helped the wife by shopping for her (in Category I families husbands frequently did the shopping not in order to help their wives but because they controlled the money). He also helped to clean the house and tidy the garden, etc. Her parents lived together in the same house in Chimbu, so wife S was used to this arrangement, and thought it superior to the traditional system of separate houses for husbands and wives.

Length of stay in   Husband: 1 year; wife: 1 year.
Port Moresby:

Notes: Implicit in the wife's father's allowing his daughter to marry without brideprice as the young man was a student, was the notion that among educated families young men are expected to pay brideprice themselves for their wife. Husband R saved up and paid for his own wife, as did husband T. Chimbu regard educated young men as outside the traditional exchange system of their kin.[1]

The young wife was the best educated of all the wives in my sample, but she was very retiring and scarcely talked when her husband was present. When I talked to her on her own she was co-operative, shared many interesting thoughts, spoke in English and had strong emotional feelings for both her mother and her husband.

This couple socialised with New Guinean members of their church (few, if any, Papuans were members of the Lutheran church) of all education and income levels. Their best friends were couple G, followed by couple R. The husband also had many 'formal' social relationships. He said he did not know much about Chimbu or European traditions. Both husband and wife worried about a shortage of money and the expense of living in Port Moresby.

Family T

Education level: Husband: Form 3 and on-the-job training. He spent six months training in Australia. He lived at home until he went to secondary school.

Wife: Form 1. Began tertiary training, but did not complete it.

Residence: a) Place: Initially in an intermediate house, but later they moved into a high-cost housing suburb nearer where the husband worked.

b) Type of house: The first house was a three-bedroomed fibro house with power, running hot and cold water, flush toilet and drainage. The second house was a large, old wooden house, also with power, running hot and cold water and flush toilet. In both houses the basic items of furniture were provided.

Husband's work: Senior administrative officer.

Wife's work: Housework and dressmaking.

Type of marriage: a) Method of marriage: After considerable opposition from the wife's family, the couple obtained their permission to marry, which in this case simply meant setting up a home together. There was no brideprice paid until about four years later, when the husband, he claimed of his own volition, paid brideprice to the wife's family to 'keep them happy'. His uncle helped him, but the major contribution was made by the husband.

---

[1] In the Motuan villages around Port Moresby where today nearly all young men are educated, the young men's kin group contributes towards payment for a bride for him. This places the husband under an obligation to these relatives, and over the years he must pay back his 'debt' by contributing towards their traditional brideprice or other payments. Perhaps this is why families protest if educated Motuans are transferred away from Port Moresby by their employer (Belshaw 1957). The Chimbu appear to have developed a different system.

b) **Present conjugal relationship:** Joint. The husband wanted very much to have a companionate type of marriage, and was an astute observer of expatriate family life. He helped his wife in the home and most leisure-time activities were carried out as a family. The wife was well satisfied with this approach. Both husband and wife were extremely ambitious for their children. However different aspects of traditional attitudes and practices pulled them in different directions, so mutual tolerance was required in this conjugal relationship.

Length of stay in   Husband: 3 years; wife: 3 years.
Port Moresby:

Notes: In spite of his relatively high income this husband seemed to be continually worried about not having sufficient money either now or in the future. Related to this was his concern that his wife did not have enough education to be able to obtain a good job (she did not want one at the moment, but the husband was looking to the future when the children were at school).

Bibliography

Bailey, K.V. and Whiteman, J., 1963. 'Dietary studies among the Chimbu (New Guinea highlands)', Trop. Geogr. Med., vol. 15, pp.377-88.

Barnett, T.E. ed., 1970. 'Case book on the Formation of Customary Marriage in selected areas of Papua and New Guinea', mimeographed, Administrative College, Waigani.

Barnes, J.A., 1972. Social networks, Addison-Wesley Module in Anthropology no.26, Reading, Mass.

Bar-Yosef, R.W., 1970. 'Cultural differences and role differentiation in urban families in Israel', mimeographed paper given at the Eleventh International Family Research Seminar, London.

Blood, R.O. and Wolfe, D.M., 1960. Husbands and Wives, Glencoe Free Press.

Bott, E., 1971. Family and Social Network, Tavistock Publications, London, second (and enlarged) edition.

Brookfield, H. and Brown, P., 1963. Struggle for Land, Oxford University Press, London.

Brown, P., 1964. 'Enemies and affines', Ethnology, vol.3, no.4, pp.335-56.

-- 1969. 'Marriage in Chimbu' in Pigs, Pearlshells and Women (R.M. Glasse and M.J. Meggitt, eds), pp.79-95, Prentice-Hall, Englewood Cliffs, N.J.

-- 1972. The Chimbu: A Study of Change in the New Guinea Highlands, Schenkman Publishing Company Cambridge, Mass.

Clignet, R. and Sween, J., 1969. 'Social change and type of marriage', American Journal of Sociology, vol.75, no.1, pp.123-45.

Department of External Territories, Statistics Section, 1971. Compendium of Statistics for Papua and New Guinea, Canberra.

Fielding, W.J., 1942. Strange Customs of Courtship and Marriage, The Blakiston Company, Philadelphia.

Harrell-Bond, B.E., 1969. 'Conjugal role behaviour', Human Relations, vol.22, pp.77-91.

Hatanaka, S., 1972. 'Leaderships and socio-economic change in Sinasina, New Guinea highlands', New Guinea Research Bulletin no.45, New Guinea Research Unit, Port Moresby and Canberra.

Keys, A., et al.,1950. Human Starvation, North Central Publishing Company, St Paul, Minnesota.

Kiki, A.M. and Beier, U., 1969. 'Women of Orokolo', Journal of the Papua and New Guinea Society, vol.3, no.1, pp.14-20.

Langness, L.L., 1969. 'Marriage in Bena Bena' in Pigs, Pearlshells and Women (R.M. Glasse and M.J. Meggitt, eds), pp.38-55, Prentice Hall, Englewood Cliffs, N.J.

Lind, A.W., 1969. 'Inter-ethnic marriage in New Guinea', New Guinea Research Bulletin no.31, New Guinea Research Unit, Port Moresby and Canberra.

Little, K., 1962. 'Some traditionally based forms of mutual aid in West African urbanisation', Ethnology, vol.1, no.2, pp.197-211.

Marwick, M.G., 1965. Sorcery and Its Social Setting; A study of the Northern Rhodesian Cewa, Manchester University Press, Manchester.

Meggitt, M.J., 1964. 'Male-female relationships in the highlands of Australian New Guinea', American Anthropologist, vol.66, no.4, part 2, pp.204-24.

Mogey, J.M., 1956. Family and Neighbourhood, Oxford University Press, London.

Nadel, S.F., 1952. 'Witchcraft in four African societies', American Anthropologist, vol.54, no.1, pp.18-29.

Nilles, J., 1950. 'The Kuman of the Chimbu Region, Central Highlands, New Guinea', Oceania, vol.21, no.1, pp.25-65.

-- 1953. 'The Kuman people: a study of cultural change in a primitive society in the Central Highlands of New Guinea', Oceania, vol.24, no.1, pp.1-27; and no.2, pp.119-31.

Oeser, L., 1969. 'Hohola: The significance of social networks in urban adaptation of women in Papua-New Guinea's first low-cost housing estate', New Guinea Research Bulletin no.29, New Guinea Research Unit, Port Moresby and Canberra.

Oram, N., 1968. 'Culture change, economic development and migration among the Hula', Oceania, vol.38, no.4, pp.243-75.

-- 'The Hula in Port Moresby', Oceania, vol.39, no.1, pp.1-35.

Phillips, A., 1953. A Survey of African Marriage and Family Life, printed by the Oxford University Press for the International African Institute.

Radcliffe-Brown, A.R., and Forde, D., eds. 1950. African Systems of Kinship and Marriage, Oxford University Press, London.

Reay, M., 1959. The Kuma: Freedom and Conformity in the New Guinea Highlands. Melbourne University Press, Melbourne.

Ross, J.A., 1965. 'The puberty ceremony of the Chimbu girl in the Eastern Highlands of New Guinea', Anthropos, vol.60, pp.423-32.

Strathern, M., 1972. Women in Between. Female Roles in a Male World: Mount Hagen, New Guinea, Seminar Press, London.

Turner, C., 1967. 'Conjugal roles and social networks: a re-examination of an hypothesis', Human Relations, vol.20, pp.221-30.

-- 1969. Family and Kinship in Modern Britain, Routledge and Kegan Paul, London.

Ward, R.G., and Lea, D.A.M. eds, 1970. An Atlas of Papua New Guinea, University of Papua and New Guinea and Collins-Longman, Hong Kong.

Whiteman, J., 1965. 'Girls' puberty ceremonies amongst the Chimbu', Anthropos, vol.60, pp.410-22.

Yeld, E.R., 1967. 'Continuity and change in Kiga patterns of marriage: an analysis of structural change in Kiga marriage in the 1930s and the 1960s', Makerere Institute of Social Research, Conference Papers, January 1967, roneoed.

Adoption, 13, 87
Affection, in marriage, 36, 37
Army, family life in the, 5, 7n, 78
Arranged marriages, mission
 opposition to, 27

Bott, E., study of social networks
 and conjugal role-relationships,
 1-2, 8; applicability of present
 study to, 145-6
Breastfeeding, abstinence from sexual
 intercourse during, 31, 32
Brideprice, 22, 24, 28-9, 35, 42n,
 81, 82, 89, 121, 137
Brothers, role of, 22n, 33, 34, 107
'Bundling', 28n

Card-playing, 69n, 72, 74, 79, 93;
 see also Gambling
Catholic mission: opposition to
 arranged marriages, 27; opposition
 to polygyny, 21
Catholics, in sample, 8
Character, Chimbu, 13
Child care: by social category I
 parents, 55-8, 64; by social category II parents, 76; by social
 category III parents, 84; social
 categories in Port Moresby compared, 110-13, 141-2; traditional,
 33-5, 57
Children, 89n; fathers' attitudes to,
 31, 33; importance of, 30, 114,
 135, 136; ownership of, on divorce
 of parents, 28-9; spacing of, 31;
 women blamed for failure to produce,
 21; women's attitudes to, 32, 33
Chimbu, defined, 10
'Chimbu proper', 10; women's houses
 in, 16
Christians, 81; attitude to polygyny,
 22, 127; see also Catholics;
 Lutherans
Chuave, 10
Clothing, traditional, 17
Coffee, 14, 14n
Complementary conjugal activities in
 Port Moresby, 104, 105, 108, 110-11,
 112; of London families, 39, 40; of
 traditional Chimbu, 40-1
Conjugal activities: see Complementary
 conjugal activities; Independent
 conjugal activities; Joint conjugal
 activities

Conjugal role-relationships, 9; individual variations in, 37; organisation of activities, 136-7; social
 category I, 67, 72, 74-5; social
 category II, 80; social category III,
 82-3, 86, 89-91; traditional, 40-1,
 135-7; see also Child care; Division
 of labour; Domestic work; Financial
 arrangements; Husband wife relations;
 Husbands, characteristics of good;
 Leisure activities; Marriage, Chimbu
 reasons for; Polygyny; Separation
 of husband and wife, reasons for;
 Sexual relations; Witchcraft
Consummation of marriage, 23,30
Contraception: traditional, 32; see
 also Family planning
Cooking: in Chimbu, 18-20; in Port
 Moresby, 53, 54-5
Courting activities: in Chimbu, 26,
 27-8; in Port Moresby, 27n
Co-wives, relations between, 32
Cultivation practices: traditional,
 14; see also Gardening
Customs, 11

Decision-making: in Port Moresby, 57,
 90, 113; traditional, 13, 37
Diet, 14, 31n
Division of labour: in Port Moresby,
 130, 132; traditional, 4, 108, 135,
 136
Divorce, traditional, 28-9
Domestic life: social category I,
 51-2, 53, 54, 55; social category
 II, 76; social category III, 91;
 traditional, 15-20
Domestic work, as measure of conjugal
 role segregation, 107-10
Drinking (alcohol), 34,53,88,138n

Economic factors, importance in conjugal relationship, 20, 21n, 25, 32,
 41, 123, 127; see also Brideprice;
 Financial arrangements
Education: social category I attitudes
 to, 57, 60; social category III
 attitudes to, 84
Elimbaris, 10
Emotional satisfaction, in marriage,
 25-6, 32, 37, 67, 74, 123, 136;
 see also Affection; Love
Exogamy, 22-3, 26

174

External relationships: traditional, 36; see also Formal external relationships

Family life: in urban areas, 4; in tribal societies, 4, 36-7; see also Domestic life

Family planning, 91; see also Contraception

Financial arrangements: as measure of domestic organisation, 104-7; social category I, 62-3; social category III, 88; see also Kampani

Food money: social category I, 58, 63, 139, 140

Formal external relationships, 96-8; social category I, 58-9, 74; social category II, 79; social category III, 86, 91-2

Gambling: in Chimbu, 20, 35; in Port Moresby, 53, 58, 63, 88, 139

Gardening: in Chimbu, 18; in Port Moresby, 66, 67, 132n, 140

Gossip, as traditional means of social control, 32

Gumine, 10; marriage ceremonies, 25; ownership of children, 28; people in Port Moresby, 68-9; women's houses, 16-17

Highlands Highway, 11, 15

Home area, attitudes to, 144-5

House: attitudes of couples sleeping in same, 125, 127; see also Men's houses; Women's houses

Household items, in Chimbu, 14

Housing: social category I, 51, 60; social category II, 76; social category III, 80

Hula, 13

Husband-wife relations: in Chimbu, 31, 36; see also Conjugal role-relationships

Husbands: characteristics of good, 89, 90, 119; social category I, 51, 140; traditional responsibilities, 36; traditional social networks, 41-2

Independent conjugal activities: in Port Moresby, 103, 104, 105, 110, 113, 116; of London families, 39, 40; of traditional Chimbu families, 40-41

Initiation ceremonies, 35; see also Puberty rites

Insecurity, wives' feelings of, in Port Moresby, 127, 138, 141

Interviews, 8-9

Joint conjugal activities: in Port Moresby, 103, 104, 105, 108, 111, 112, 114, 116; of London families, 39, 40; of traditional Chimbu families, 40-1

Kampani, 62, 63, 88, 105-7

Kin, relationships with, 46-7, 136-7; effect of witchcraft on, 129-30; social category I, 61, 79, 85, 99, 101; social category II, 76, 78, 79, 99, 101; social category III, 80, 85, 88, 101

Kinship terms, difficulties in the use of, 93-4

Kuma, 16n; arranged marriages, 26

Kundiawa, 11, 14, 15

Land in Chimbu, rights to, 61n, 80

Leadership, traditional, 13

Learning, traditional methods of, 34

Leisure activities: in Port Moresby 113-4; traditional, 113

Love, as element in marriage, 84; see also Emotional satisfaction, in marriage

Lutheran mission; opposition to traditional courting practices, 27; opposition to polygyny, 21

Lutherans, in sample, 8

Marriage: breakdown, 28; Chimbu reasons for, 119, 121, 123; pragmatic Chimbu view of, 83-4; traditional, 20-7, 135-7, 141; see also Brideprice; Divorce; Economic factors, importance in conjugal relations; Emotional satisfaction, in marriage; Polygyny; Sexual satisfaction, in marriage

Marriage history: social category I, 68; social category III, 80, 81, 89

Melpa, 16n, 26n, 66n

Men: attitudes to women, 15-16, 29-37; clothing, 17; domestic life in Chimbu, 16, 17, 20; see also Husbands

Men's houses, 15, 16

Method of study, 6-9

Migration to urban areas, reasons for, 6

Missions, see Catholic mission; Lutheran mission

Mobility, geographic, 6, 49

Neighbours, relationships with, 78-9, 94-5

Non-Chimbu, relationships with, 78; see also Papuans

Papuans, relationships with, 62, 64, 67, 69-70, 70n, 73-4, 79, 98, 99, 138

Personal allowances: social category I, 58, 63, 140; social category II, 58n, 63; social category III, 58n, 88

Physical conditions, Chimbu, 14-15

Pig festivals, 15, 16, 27

Pigs, 16; women's task to look after, 20

Polygyny: as traditional ideal, 20-1
136; attitudes to, 127, 129; mission
opposition to, 21; social category
I attitudes to, 59, 71, 84; social
category II attitudes to, 76, 78;
social category III attitudes to,
82-4
Port Moresby: housing, 5; population,
5
Pregnancy: abstinence from sexual
intercourse during, 31, 32; of single
girl, 36
Premarital sexual relations, 29-30, 36
Prostitution, 138n, 141n, 144
Puberty rites: in Chimbu, 34; in Port
Moresby, 68-9n, 70n; see also
Initiation ceremonies

Quarrels, marital, 65-6, 127, 130, 138,
140; settlement of, 28, 140n

Reciprocity, 14, 47, 129
Religion: influence on life-style, 49;
see also Christians
Residential pattern, traditional, 11,
15

Sample: characteristics of, 6-7; selection of, 7
Segregation of roles, traditional, 36-7,
42
Separation of husband and wife, reasons
for, 123, 125
Sexual relations., 125n; abstinence during pregnancy and breastfeeding, 31,
32; Bott's study of, 114-6; in Port
Moresby, 66, 67, 114, 116, 141; traditional, 13n, 15, 16, 29-33, 37,
136
Sexual satisfaction, in marriage, 29,
30, 32, 37, 67, 114-6, 116
Sinasina, 10, 11; ownership of children, 28
Social categories, basis of classification, 45-7, 137
Social category I families, 47; attitudes to children, 57-8, 64; attitudes to education, 57, 60; case-
studies, 59-75; domestic life, 51,
53, 54-5, 55; education, 51; financial arrangements, 62-3; food money,
58; formal external relationships,
58-9; gambling, 53, 58; housing,
51, 60; mobility, 49; personal
allowances, 58; religion, 49;
social networks, 137-8
Social category II families, 47; attitude to children, 142; conjugal
relationships, 142,166; domestic life,
76, 108; mobility, 49; polygyny, 76,
77; religion, 49; social networks,
78-9, 142

Social category III families, 47,
47-8; case-study, 86-92; child care,
142-3; conjugal role-relationships,
143; education, 80; housing, 80;
mobility, 49; religion, 49; social
networks, 142-3
Social class, applicability of term to
Chimbu in Port Moresby, 43-5
Social control, traditional means of,
32-3
Social networks, 9; Bott's use of terms
concerning, 39; qualitative analysis
of, 9, 101-2; social category I, 68-
71, 73-5, 93, 99, 101; social category II, 78-9, 93, 99, 101; social
category III, 86, 91-2, 94, 101;
traditional Chimbu, 41-2, 93; see
also Social category I; Social
category II; Social category III
Status: in Port Moresby, 43-5; traditional, 43
Subclans, 15

'Turning head' parties, 27, 28

Wandi, 14, 17n
Warfare, traditional, 13
Witchcraft (sanguma) 33, 46, 54-5, 72,
78, 92, 129-30
Wives: attitudes to polygyny, 127, 129;
attitudes to urban life, 53, 55, 66,
67, 142-3, 144; characteristics of
good, 89, 90, 117, 119; control over
own income, 63, 72, 104, 140; domestic activities, 53, 54; economic
dependence on husbands, 66, 105,
139-40; gambling, 140, 141; husbands'
limited need of in Port Moresby, 141;
lack of gardening in Port Moresby,
66, 67, 132n, 140; lack of opportunities in Port Moresby, 132, 139; lack
of personal allowance, 140; marital
duties, 110, 140; reasons for coming
to Port Moresby, 139n; social networks,
70-1; traditional lack of recreation,
113; traditional responsibilities, 20,
36; traditional social networks, 41-2,
117
Women: attitude to men, 29; benefits of
marriage for, 136; changing role of,
37n; clothing, 17; domestic life in
Chimbu, 16, 17, 18-20; earnings from
market, 14; traditional decision-
making, 13; see also Wives
Women's houses, 15, 16

Abstract

New Guinea Research Bulletin
No.52, 1973

Chimbu family relation-
ships in Port Moresby,
by J. Whiteman

Modern, urban conditions in Port
Moresby present problems of adaptation
to Chimbu families who, from individual
choice, force of circumstances, or both,
do not practise traditional domestic and
family organisation in the city. This
study, based upon one made by Bott et al
in London, discusses traditional family
life in Chimbu and explores and analyses
the conjugal relationships and social
networks of twenty Chimbu families living in Port Moresby.

New Guinea Research Bulletins

Bulletin No. 1   The Erap Mechanical Farming Project by R.G. Crocombe and
                  G.R. Hogbin, April 1963

Bulletin No. 2   Land, Work and Productivity at Inonda by R.G. Crocombe and
                  G.R. Hogbin, August 1963

Bulletin No. 3   Social Accounts of the Monetary Sector of the Territory of
                  Papua and New Guinea, 1956/57 to 1960/61 by R.C. White,
                  January 1964

Bulletin No. 4   Communal Cash Cropping among the Orokaiva by R.G. Crocombe,
                  May 1964

Bulletin No. 5   A Survey of Indigenous Rubber Producers in the Kerema Bay
                  Area by G.R. Hogbin, October 1964

Bulletin No. 6   The European Land Settlement Scheme at Popondetta by
                  D.R. Howlett, April 1965

Bulletin No. 7   The M'buke Co-operative Plantation by R.G. Crocombe,
                  August 1965

Bulletin No. 8   Cattle, Coffee and Land among the Wain by Graham Jackson,
                  December 1965

Bulletin No. 9   An Integrated Approach to Nutrition and Society: the case
                  of the Chimbu, ed. E. Hipsley, January 1966

Bulletin No.10   The Silanga Resettlement Project by Olga van Rijswijck,
                  February 1966

Bulletin No.11   Land Tenure and Land Use among the Mount Lamington
                  Orokaiva by Max Rimoldi, April 1966

Bulletin No.12   Education Through the Eyes of an Indigenous Urban Elite by
                  Karol van der Veur and Penelope Richardson, August 1966

Bulletin No.13   Orokaiva Papers: Miscellaneous Papers on the Orokaiva of
                  North East Papua, November 1966

Bulletin No.14   Rabia Camp: a Port Moresby Migrant Settlement by Nancy E.
                  Hitchcock and N.D. Oram, January 1967

Bulletin No.15   Bulolo: a History of the Development of the Bulolo Region,
                  New Guinea by Allan Healy, February 1967

Bulletin No.16   Papuan Entrepreneurs: Papers by R.G. Crocombe, W.J. Ooster-
                  meyer and Joanne Gray, J.V. Langmore, April 1967

Bulletin No.17   Land Tenure Conversion in the Northern District of Papua
                  by David Morawetz, May 1967

Bulletin No.18   Social and Economic Relationships in a Port Moresby Canoe
                  Settlement by N.D. Oram, July 1967

Bulletin No.19   A Benefit Cost Analysis of Resettlement in the Gazelle
                  Peninsula by S. Singh, September 1967

Bulletin No.20   New Guinea People in Business and Industry: Papers from the
                  First Waigani Seminar, December 1967

178

Bulletin No.21   Teachers in the Urban Community by Penelope Richardson and Karol van der Veur, January 1968

Bulletin No.22   Papers on the Papua-New Guinea House of Assembly by Norman Meller, January 1968

Bulletin No.23   Mixed-race Society in Port Moresby by B.G. Burton-Bradley, March 1968

Bulletin No.24   The Organisation of Production and Distribution among the Orokaiva by E.W. Waddell and P.A. Krinks, September 1968

Bulletin No.25   A Survey of Village Industries in Papua-New Guinea by R. Kent Wilson, November 1968

Bulletin No.26   The Contribution of Voluntary Aid Organisations to the Development of Papua-New Guinea, 1966-67, by Micheline Dewdney, January 1969

Bulletin No.27   New Guinean Entrepreneurs by B.R. Finney, February 1969

Bulletin No.28   Namasu: New Guinea's Largest Indigenous-owned Company by I.J. Fairbairn, March 1969

Bulletin No.29   Hohola: the Significance of Social Networks in Urban Adaptation of Women by Lynn Oeser, June 1969

Bulletin No.30   Inter-tribal Relations of the Maenge People of New Britain by M. Panoff, July 1969

Bulletin No.31   Inter-ethnic Marriage in New Guinea by A.W. Lind, August 1969

Bulletin No.32   New Guinea Social Science Field Research and Publications, 1962-67 by Susan C. Reeves and May Dudley, October 1969

Bulletin No.33   The Rigo Road: a Study of the Economic Effects of New Road Construction by Marion W. Ward, January 1970

Bulletin No.34   People and Planning in Papua and New Guinea: Papers by D.J. van de Kaa, J.M. Stanhope, T.S. Epstein, N.H. Fry, and C.L. Beltz, April 1970

Bulletin No.35   The Indigenous Role in Business Enterprise: Three Papers from the Third Waigani Seminar, 1969 by A.J. O'Connor, T.S. Epstein and G. Nash, May 1970

Bulletin No.36   Australia and the United Nations: New Guinea Trusteeship Issues from 1946 to 1966 by W.E. Thomasetti, July 1970

Bulletin No.37   Port Moresby Urban Development by J.V. Langmore and N.D. Oram, September 1970

Bulletin No.38   Land Tenure in West Irian: Papers by K.W. Galis, J.V. de Bruyn, J. Pouwer, J.W. Schoorl, and J. Verschueren, December 1970

Bulletin No.39   The Situm and Gobari Ex-servicemen's Settlements by A. Ploeg, January 1971

Bulletin No.40   Land Tenure and Economic Development: Problems and Policies in New Guinea and Kenya: Papers by S. Rowton Simpson, R.L. Hide, A.M. Healy, and J.K. Kinyanjui, March 1971

Bulletin No.41   Would-be Entrepreneurs? A Study of Motivation in New Guinea by Ruth S. Finney, May 1971

Bulletin No.42   Population Growth and Socio-economic Change: Papers from the Second Demography Seminar, Port Moresby 1970, September 1971

Bulletin No.43   Langandrowa and M'buke, Corporate Indigenous Plantations by
                 A.M. McGregor, December 1971

Bulletin No.44   Business and Cargo: Socio-economic change among the Nasioi of
                 Bougainville by E. Ogan, 1972

Bulletin No.45   Leadership and Socio-economic Change in Sinasina by Sachiko
                 Hatanaka, 1972

Bulletin No.46   Melanesians' Choice: Tadhimboko Participation in the Solomon
                 Islands Cash Economy by I.Q. Lasaqa, 1972

Bulletin No.47   Official and Unofficial Courts: Legal Assumptions and Expecta-
                 tions in a Highlands Community by Marilyn Strathern, 1972

Bulletin No.48   Freight Forwarding in the Australia-Papua New Guinea Trade by
                 P.J. Rimmer, 1972

Bulletin No.49   Hoskins Development: the Role of Oil Palm and Timber - Papers
                 by J.P. Longayroux, T. Fleming, A. Ploeg, R.T. Shand and
                 W.F. Straatmans, and W. Jonas, 1973

Bulletin No.50   The Land Titles Commission in Chimbu: an Analysis of Colonial
                 Land Law and Practice, 1933-68 by R. Hide, 1973

Bulletin No.51   Constitutional Development in Papua New Guinea, 1968-73: the
                 Transfer of Executive Power by P.J. Bayne and H.K. Colebatch,
                 1973

Bulletin No.52   Chimbu Conjugal Relationships in Port Moresby by J. Whiteman,
                 1973

The above bulletins are available at $1.50 until 1974, when they will cost
$2.00 each, from the A.N.U Press, The Australian National University, P.O. Box 4,
Canberra, A.C.T., 2600, Australia, and the New Guinea Research Unit, The Australian
National University, P.O. Box 1238, Boroko, Papua New Guinea.

An annual payment of $10 entitles the subscriber to all bulletins issued in
the year.